C000260651

THE FINEST GARDENS IN WALES

After studying forestry and horticulture in the early 1980s, Tony Russell's career with plants has taken him from Snowdonia to the New Forest in Hampshire, then to Westonbirt Arboretum in Gloucestershire (where he was Head Forester for 13 years) and recently back to Snowdonia. Tony is a familiar face and voice on TV and radio, presenting a number of TV series such as *Garden Trail, Roots & Shoots, Britain's Great Trees, Saving Lullingstone Castle* and featuring on BBC Radio 4 in series such as *Invasive Plants* and on *Gardeners' Question Time*. He is also a regular contributor to the gardening pages of national newspapers such as *The Telegraph* and national magazines such as *BBC Gardeners' World Magazine*.

The Finest Gardens in Wales is Tony's fourteenth book and follows on from such bestselling titles as *The World Encyclopaedia of Trees, Cornwall's Great Gardens, Westonbirt – A Celebration of the Seasons, Tree Spotting for Children* and *The Cotswolds' Finest Gardens*. He is also editor of the annual publication *Great Gardens to Visit* and the magazine *Discover Britain's Gardens*.

In addition to his broadcasting and writing, Tony runs a thriving consultancy which provides advice and guidance on gardens to private owners, charitable trusts and UK-wide organisations such as the National Trust. Tony is an avid botanical traveller and regularly leads tours for plant and garden enthusiasts to locations across the world, including the Himalayas, Amazonia, China, Japan, New Zealand and India.

For more information visit:
www.gardenstovisit.net
www.amberley-books.com

THE FINEST GARDENS IN WALES

TONY RUSSELL

AMBERLEY

Dyffryn Pompeian Italian Garden

This edition first published 2015

Amberley Publishing
The Hill, Stroud
Gloucestershire, GL5 4EP
www.amberley-books.com

ISBN 978 1 4456 4125 6 (print)
ISBN 978 1 4456 4137 9 (ebook)

British Library Cataloguing in Publication Data.
A catalogue record for this book is available from the British Library.

Printed in the UK.

Photo page 1 – Plas Tan y Bwlch

INTRODUCTION

It was May 1971 when I first set foot in Wales – Snowdonia to be precise – and I came as a young fit lad on a school trip from my home in South London. Over forty years later, I can still clearly remember that astonishing first view of the mountains as my classmates and I tumbled out of the minibus above Nant Gwynant valley. Until that moment in my life, the highest 'peak' I had looked down from had been Box Hill in Surrey – a 'mighty' 735 ft (224 m) above sea level. Now I was surrounded by rugged, rocky tops up to almost five times that height. In that instant I was smitten and somehow knew my life had changed forever. By the end of the 1970s, I was living in Wales, climbing the hills during my leisure time and earning a living from my other passion – plants, gardens and trees.

My introduction to Wales will be a familiar one to many; I was initially drawn to the area by its beauty – its mountains, lakes, forests and stunning coastline – and then discovering its people, culture and heritage. Relatively few of us, however, are initially drawn to Wales because of its gardens in the way that people are drawn to Cornwall. In recent years, Cornwall's abundance of gardens have become almost as well known as its coastline; not so Wales, and yet within the boundaries of this wonderful country are some of the finest gardens to be found anywhere within the British Isles.

This book uses words and imagery to convey to the world that Wales is a place full of remarkable gardens – landscapes that represent virtually every style of garden design and every period of garden history from medieval monastic gardens through to those of the twenty-first century. Within this book you will find gardens that contain plants from every corner of the globe, including many sub-tropical plants which thrive in the mild western coastal fringes of Wales.

All of the gardens featured within this book allow public access, at least for some period during each year. I make no apologies for the final selection; they are for me the finest of their genre and tell the tale well. You, the reader and garden visitor, will judge if that is the case.

So please enjoy this book and the stories it contains, and then go out and visit the finest gardens that Wales has to offer. You will, I am sure, be enthralled and captivated.

Tony Russell
2015

THE LIST OF GARDENS

- The Hall at Abbey-Cwm-Hir 11
- Aberglasney 14
- Bodnant Garden 17
- Bodrhyddan Hall 20
- Bodysgallen Hall 23
- Bro Meigan 26
- Bryngwyn Hall 29
- Cae Hir Gardens 32
- Caerau Uchaf Gardens 35
- Centre for Alternative Technology 39
- Chirk Castle 42
- Clyne Gardens 45
- Conwy Valley Maze 48
- Cowbridge Physic Garden 51
- Crug Farm Plants 54
- Dewstow 57
- Dingle Garden 60
- Dyffryn Gardens and Arboretum 63
- Erddig 66
- Glansevern Hall Gardens 69
- Glynllifon 72
- Gregynog 75
- Gwydir Castle 78
- High Glanau Manor 81
- Llanerchaeron 84
- Llanllyr 87

THE LIST OF GARDENS

- National Botanic Garden of Wales 90
- Penpergwm Lodge 93
- Penrhyn Castle 96
- Picton Castle 99
- Plantasia 102
- Plas Brondanw 105
- Plas Cadnant 109
- Plas Newydd 112
- Plas Newydd Llangollen 115
- Plas Tan y Bwlch 118
- Plas yn Rhiw 122
- Portmeirion 125
- Powis Castle 128
- Ridler's Garden 132
- Singleton Botanical Gardens 134
- St Fagans Castle Gardens 137
- The Garden House 141
- Treborth Botanic Garden 144
- Tredegar House 147
- Tretower Court 150
- Veddw House 153
- Whimble Gardens and Nursery 156
- Wyndcliffe Court 158

FEATURED GARDENS

THE HALL AT ABBEY-CWM-HIR
Abbey-Cwm-Hir, nr. Llandrindod Wells, Powys, LD1 6PH
Tel: 01597 851 727
www.abbeycwmhir.com/

ABERGLASNEY HOUSE & GARDENS
Llangathen, Carmarthenshire, SA32 8QH
Tel: 01558 668998
www.aberglasney.org

BODNANT GARDEN
Tal-y-Cafn, Nr Colwyn Bay, Conwy, LL28 5RE
Tel: 01492 650460
www.nationaltrust.org.uk/bodnant-garden

BODRHYDDAN HALL
Clwyd, LL18 5SB
Tel: 01745 590414
www.bodrhyddan.co.uk/

BODYSGALLEN HALL
Llandudno, North Wales, LL30 1RS
Tel: 01492 584 466
www.bodysgallen.com/

BRO MEIGAN
Near Boncath, Pembrokeshire, SA37 0JE
Tel: 01239 841232
www.bromeigan.co.uk/

BRYNGWYN HALL
Bwlch-y-Cibau, Llanfyllin, Powys, SY22 5LJ
Tel: 01691 648 373
www.bryngwyn.com/

CAE HIR GARDENS
Cribyn, Lampeter, SA48 7NG
Tel: 01570 471116
www.caehirgardens.com/

CAERAU UCHAF GARDENS
Sarnau, Bala, Gwynedd, LL23 7LG
Tel: 01678 530493
www.summersgardens.co.uk/

CENTRE FOR ALTERNATIVE TECHNOLOGY
Machynlleth, Powys, SY20 9AZ
Tel: 01654 705950
visit.cat.org.uk/

CHIRK CASTLE
Chirk, Wrexham, LL14 5AF
Tel: 01691 777701
www.nationaltrust.org.uk/chirk-castle/

CLYNE GARDENS
120 A4067, Swansea, SA3 5BD
Tel: 01792 401737
www.swansea.gov.uk/clyne

CONWY VALLEY MAZE
Dolgarrog, Conwy, LL32 8JX
Tel: 01492 660900
www.gardenartdirect.co.uk/

COWBRIDGE PHYSIC GARDEN
Church Street, Cowbridge, Vale of Glamorgan, CF71 7BB
Tel: 01446 773659
www.cowbridgephysicgarden.org.uk/

CRUG FARM
Griffith's Crossing, Caernarfon, Gwynedd, LL55 1TU
Tel: 01248 670232
www.crug-farm.co.uk/

DEWSTOW
Caerwent, Monmourthshire, NP26 5AH
Tel: 01291 431020
www.dewstowgardens.co.uk/

DINGLE GARDEN
Frochas, Welshpool, Powys, SY21 9JD
Tel: 01938 555145
www.dinglenurseryandgarden.co.uk/

DYFFRYN GARDENS & ARBORETUM
St Nicholas, Vale of Glamorgan, CF5 6SU
Tel: 029 2059 3328
www.nationaltrust.org.uk/dyffryn-gardens/

ERDDIG
Erddig, Wrexham, LL13 0YT
Tel: 01978 355314
www.nationaltrust.org.uk/erddig/

GLANSEVERN HALL GARDENS
Berriew, Welshpool, Powys, SY21 8AH
Tel: 01686 640644
www.glansevern.co.uk/

GLYNLLIFON
Clynnog Road, Nr. Caernarfon, LL54 5DY
Tel: 01286 831 832
www.glynllifon.co.uk/

GREGYNOG
Tregynon, Nr. Newtown, Powys, SY16 3PW
Tel: 01686 650224
www.gregynog.org/

GWYDIR CASTLE
Llanrwst, Conwy, LL26 0PN
Tel: 01492 641687
www.gwydircastle.co.uk/

HIGH GLANAU MANOR
Lydart, Monmouth, Gwent, NP25 4AD

LLANERCHAERON
Ciliau Aeron, near Aberaeron, Ceredigion, SA48 8DG
Tel: 01545 570200
www.nationaltrust.org.uk/llanerchaeron/

LLANLLYR
Lampeter, Ceredigion, SA48 8QB
Tel: 01570 470900

NATIONAL BOTANIC GARDEN OF WALES
Llanarthne, Carmarthen, SA32 8HN
Tel: 01558 667149
www.gardenofwales.org.uk/

FEATURED GARDENS

PENPERGWM LODGE
Abergavenny, Monmouthshire, NP7 9AS
Tel: 01873 840208
www.penplants.com/

PENRHYN CASTLE
Bangor, Gwynedd, LL57 4HN
Tel: 01248 353084
www.nationaltrust.org.uk/penrhyn-castle/

PICTON CASTLE
Haverfordwest, Pembrokeshire, SA62 4AS
Tel: 01437 751326
www.pictoncastle.co.uk/

PLANTASIA
Parc Tawe, Swansea, SA1 2AL
Tel: 01792 474555
www.swansea.gov.uk/plantasia

PLAS BRONDANW
Llanfrothen, Gwynedd, LL48 6SW
Tel: 01766 772772
www.plasbrondanw.com/

PLAS CADNANT
Cadnant Road, Menai Bridge, Isle of Anglesey, LL59 5NH
Tel: 01248 717174
www.plascadnantgardens.co.uk/

PLAS NEWYDD
Llanfairpwll, Anglesey, LL61 6DQ
Tel: 01248 714795
www.nationaltrust.org.uk/plas-newydd/

PLAS NEWYDD LLANGOLLEN
Hill Street, Llangollen, LL20 8AW
Tel: 01978 862834
www.denbighshire.gov.uk/en/visitor/places-to-visit/museums-and-historic-houses/plas-newydd.aspx

PLAS TAN Y BWLCH
Maentwrog, Blaenau Ffestiniog, LL41 3YU
Tel: 01766 772600
www.eryri-npa.gov.uk/study-centre/

PLAS YN RHIW
Rhiw, Pwllheli, Gwynedd, LL53 8AB
Tel: 01758 780219
www.nationaltrust.org.uk/plas-yn-rhiw/

PORTMEIRION
Minffordd, Penrhyndeudraeth, Gwynedd, LL48 6ER
Tel: 01766 770000
www.portmeirion-village.com/

POWIS CASTLE
Welshpool, Powys, SY21 8RF
Tel: 01938 551944
www.nationaltrust.org.uk/powis-castle/

RIDLER'S GARDEN
7 Saint Peter's Terrace, Cockett, Swansea, SA2 0FW
Tel: 01792 588217
www.tonyridlersgarden.co.uk/

SINGLETON BOTANICAL GARDENS
Singleton Park, Swansea, SA1 4PE
Tel: 01792 205327
www.swansea.gov.uk/botanics

ST FAGANS
St Fagans National History Museum, Cardiff, CF5 6XB
Tel: 029 2057 3500
www.museumwales.ac.uk/stfagans

THE GARDEN HOUSE
Erbistock, Clwyd, Wales, LL13 0DL
Tel: 01978 781149
www.simonwingett.com/

TREBORTH BOTANIC GARDEN
Bangor University, Bangor, Gwynedd, LL57 2RQ
Tel: 01248 353398
www.treborthbotanicgarden.org/

TREDEGAR HOUSE
Newport NP10 8YW
Tel: 01633 815880
www.nationaltrust.org.uk/tredegar-house/

TRETOWER COURT
Powys, Tretower, Crickhowell, Powys, NP8 1RD
Tel: 01874 730279
cadw.wales.gov.uk/daysout/tretowercourtandcastle/

VEDDW HOUSE
Devauden, Monmouthshire, NP16 6PH
Tel: 01291 650 836
www.veddw.com/

WHIMBLE GARDENS & NURSERY
Kinnerton, Presteigne, Powys, LD8 2PD
Tel: 01547 560 413
www.whimblegardens.co.uk/

WYNDCLIFFE COURT
Off Penterry Lane, St. Arvans, Chepstow, Monmouthshire, NP16 6EY
Tel: 01291 621242
www.wyndcliffecourt.co.uk/

THE MAP OF GARDENS

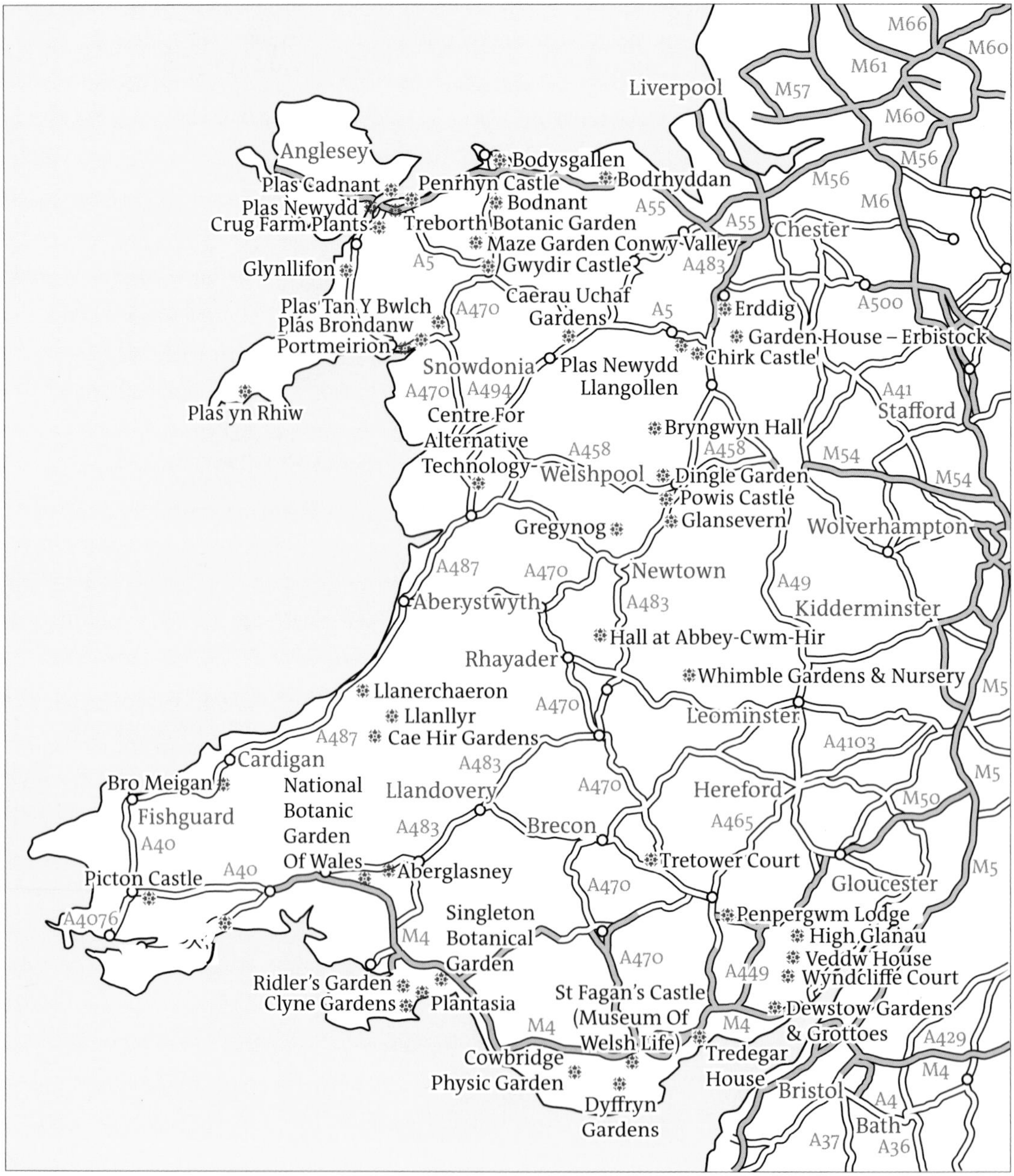

❀ THE HALL AT ABBEY-CWM-HIR

Abbey-Cwm-Hir translates from Welsh as the 'Abbey of The Long Valley'. The present property sits high above a long tree-clad valley, with views across 12 acres (4.8 hectares) of beautifully landscaped grounds and gardens, to a river, church and ruins of a twelfth-century Cistercian Abbey.

The hall itself is a 52-roomed, Grade II listed, Gothic Revival mansion, built in 1833/34 for Thomas Wilson, a London solicitor. Having financially ruined himself on the building process, the property was sold in 1837 to Francis Philips, who was a major mill owner and cotton manufacturer in the Manchester area. Eventually, the hall formed the heart of a 3,500-acre (1,416-hectare) estate, which the Philips family continued to own until 1959.

Current owners Paul and Victoria Humpherston purchased Abbey-Cwm-Hir in 1997. Within the gardens and grounds they found many features and remnants of the past, but all were in a serious state of disrepair. These included a 1 ¾-acre (0.7 hectare) walled garden, which had at one time contained peach, cucumber and mushroom houses, as well as an undersoil heating system. The sweeping lawns, terraces and courtyards were devoid of ornamental planting and swamped by nettles. A 5-acre (2-hectare) woodland was largely impenetrable due to rampant rhododendron and rose briars. ▸

Golden Irish yews and purple-leaved maples in the walled garden at Abbey-Cwm-Hir

◂ Similarly inaccessible was a lake and waterfall, originally created in the 1840s to produce power for the local village sawmill.

Undaunted, the Humpherstons immediately recognised the potential of the property and spent the next ten years restoring both hall and garden to their former glory.

Today, the walled garden is a triumph, with Paul's Celtic cross design taking centre stage. The outer circle is planted with trees and shrubs in a blue, yellow and purple theme. Here, sentinel golden Irish yews punctuate plantings of glaucous-blue prostrate junipers, while the formality is softened by purple-leaved cotinus, Japanese maples and roses. To the sides of the cross, rectangular borders flow with large-leaved hostas, nepeta, geraniums and phlox, all backed by walls bedecked in clematis, wisteria, vines and golden hop.

Beyond the garden walls, the eccentricity of this modest, lovely couple begins to creep in. Walks through the surrounding woodland reveal faithfully restored gypsy caravans, a line of beach huts, a Viking galley and a 12-foot-high brown bear! If that were not enough, the interior of the hall is quite simply a celebration of eccentricity and I defy anyone not to enjoy the tour on offer, which takes in all fifty-two rooms.

◂ Celtic cross lawn with Abbey-Cwm-Hir Hall in the background

Rhododendron lawn at Abbey-Cwm-Hir

ABERGLASNEY

Aberglasney is perhaps one of the most exciting garden restorations of the past twenty years. Its 10 acres (4 hectares) have a gardening pedigree dating back to the fifteenth century, when mention was first made in poetry of 'nine gardens, orchards and vineyards'. The astonishing survival of St David's Bishop Rudd's garden structure from 1630 makes this garden truly unique. It was he who almost certainly built the gatehouse and created the original cloister garden. Over the centuries Aberglasney has gone through ever-changing periods of wealth and prosperity followed by debt, neglect and decay. In 1995, the house was derelict and the garden lost beneath a sea of weeds. It was then that the Aberglasney Restoration Trust began its good work, backed by a donation from a wealthy American benefactor and watched by the nation through the medium of TV.

Today there are six different garden spaces, including three walled gardens. At Aberglasney's heart is the unique and fully restored Elizabethan cloister garden, surrounded on three sides by a parapet walk, a long arcaded walkway supporting a broad platform and the only surviving example of its kind in the UK. It offers excellent vantage points over the large upper walled garden, redesigned by Penelope Hobhouse to complement the historic nature of the site and consisting of classic evergreens known at the time of Bishop Rudd, including clipped box hedging. ▸

Aberglasney Cloister Garden

Aberglasney House, Terrace and Pool ▸

◀ However, within this historical structure, and in contrast, is an ornamental collection of rare and unusual perennials, climbers and shrubs of such diversity that this garden has truly developed into a modern-day plant-lover's paradise.

The lower walled garden is laid out in traditional quartered divisions and has a functional role, being given over to vegetables and herbs. It also contains a cutting garden where wide selections of annual and perennial flowering plants are grown. Historically, these plants would have been cut and used in the house both for decoration and to provide an attractive fragrance to offset the less welcome aromas of Elizabethan living.

The creation of a winter garden in 2005 called the Ninfarium (after the medieval garden near Rome) provides a further level of diversity. Situated in the ruinous central courtyard of the mansion, it displays a wonderful collection of exotic subtropical plants. To the side of the house is a rare example of an eighteenth-century yew tunnel full of gnarled and venerable forms that seem to have stepped straight out of J. R. R. Tolkien's imagination.

Aberglasney, roses in Cloister Garden

BODNANT GARDEN

Positioned high above the River Conwy on ground that slopes to the west, there are few gardens in Britain that can rival the vistas found at Bodnant. On a fine day, the views beyond Himalayan magnolias and American conifers to the hazy blue mountain ridges of Snowdonia are truly sublime.

The garden covers 80 acres (32 hectares) and owes its beginning to Henry David Pochin, who bought the estate in 1874. It was Pochin who in 1882 planted one of Bodnant's most famous features, the 180-ft-long (55-m) Laburnum Arch.

After Pochin's death in 1895, his daughter Laura inherited the estate. She was married to Charles McLaren, a barrister and Member of Parliament, who became a peer in 1911 and took as his title Aberconway (mouth of the River Conwy). Charles was not a gardener, but their son Henry was, and it was he, along with three generations of head gardeners from the same family, Frederick, Charles and Martin Puddle, who created and maintained much of the garden that can be seen today. Henry McLaren died in 1953, having donated the garden to the National Trust in 1949. The family continue to live in the house, which is not open to the public. ▸

Terrace Garden looking towards Snowdonia

◂ There are several distinct areas within Bodnant. The upper garden consists of mixed borders of summer-flowering herbaceous perennials, lawns shaded by ancient sweet chestnuts and Monterey pines and island beds planted with spring-flowering shrubs. West of the house, a series of five formal terraces descend steeply in the direction of the distant mountains. There are two rose terraces, a Baroque French fountain and croquet terrace, a lily pool terrace and a stunning Dutch-influenced Canal Terrace. At the southern end of the rectangular canal stands the Pin Mill, a white stuccoed building of unique beauty. Originally built in 1730 in Woodchester, Gloucestershire, it was seen in 1938 by the 2nd Lord Aberconway in a rapid state of decay; he bought it, rescued it and rebuilt it at Bodnant.

Beyond the Pin Mill, the garden descends into 'The Dell', a steep-sided valley containing the fast-running River Hiraethlyn. Here a collection of mature shrubs, particularly rhododendrons and azaleas, shelter beneath canopies of magnolias and maples, which are in turn shaded by tall gun-barrel-straight pine, spruce and fir. Planted in 1874, these trees now rise like arboreal giants above the valley floor, which is rather apt considering Bodnant's status as one of the giants of the horticultural world.

◂ The Dell in springtime

The laburnum arch at Bodnant

BODRHYDDAN HALL

Boddrhyddan Hall, with its fine Grade II listed Welsh Historic Garden, has been owned by the Langford family for 500 years. It is currently home to Geoffery Alexander Rowley-Conwy, the 9th Baron Langford, and his wife, Lady Susan Langford. It is situated 4 miles (6.4km) south-east of the seaside resort of Rhyl on the North Wales coast.

The hall itself is a seventeenth-century house, built on the site of an earlier timber-framed wattle and daub building, with Queen Anne revival additions and alterations carried out in 1875 by the renowned architect William Eden Nesfield.

The gardens surrounding the property extend to around 8 acres (3.2 hectares) and are a delightful mix of formal and informal designs. Immediately to the south-east of the hall is probably Bodrhyddan's most famous garden feature, an intricate box-edged parterre laid out by William Andrews Nesfield, father of architect William Eden Nesfield. It has at its centre a fountain pool with complementing stork-carried planters at either end. Within the evergreen foil of the box hedging, bedding schemes, sometimes of geraniums and ageratum, produce summer-long tapestry patterns of red, blue or white, which reach their best in late July. ▸

Bodryhddan lake and bridge

The Pleasance and Millennium Summerhouse ▸

◂ The paths leading to the parterre are bordered by centuries-old clipped yew pillars, which today, like aged but distinguished gentlemen, sag and lean at jaunty angles, or throw out arched branches to their venerable companions in a way that suggests they have their arms around each other's shoulders for support.

Eastwards from the parterre lies the old park with its brick-walled kitchen garden and ice house, and to the north-west is the 2-acre (0.8-hectare) Pleasance, a woodland garden which was once part of a much larger area known as The Grove. Here, beneath a 1612 Inigo Jones pavilion, said to have been used for clandestine weddings, lies St Mary's Well, a source of fresh water dating back to pagan times. By the nineteenth century, this area was given over to a Victorian shrubbery, but a restoration, which began in 1983, has led today to a vibrant and interesting garden of island beds, serpentine lawns dotted with trees and shrubs, and tranquil pools fringed by large-leaved foliage plants, flowering hydrangeas and spanned by Giverny-style bridges. At the furthest point of the vista, placed upon rising ground that gives way to woodland, is a Millennium-built summerhouse, inspired architecturally by the Treasury at Petra, upon which the present Lord Langford's great-great-grand-parents inscribed their names when on honeymoon in 1835.

Bodrhyddan parterre

BODYSGALLEN HALL

Positioned high on the limestone escarpment of Bryn Pydew, Bodysgallen Hall is approached across 200 acres (81 hectares) of rolling parkland grazed by sheep and dotted with ancient Welsh oaks, ash and the occasional mature elm that has escaped the attention of the disease-bearing bark beetle *Scolytus scolytus*; all remnants no doubt from the sylvan scene that met Welsh naturalist and writer Thomas Pennant in 1781, and then Richard Fenton when he visited here in 1810 and remarked that Bodysgallen was 'embosomed in woods of noble growth'.

Bodysgallen was originally built in 1250 as an outlying watchtower to Conwy Castle, which lies less than 2 miles away and can be viewed from the Terrace Walk beyond the garden. In 1620 (and then again in 1900), the original tower was extended into the present Grade I Listed hall, which is now one of three historic house hotels owned by the National Trust. From the hall there are views to Great and Little Orme on the North Wales coastline and south-west to the mountains of Snowdonia.

Below the hall a series of historic gardens includes a rare example of a seventeenth-century 'gay parterre' (colourful pattern) comprised of clipped box hedges filled with herbs. ▸

The seventeenth-century parterre at Bodysgallen

❁ BODYSGALLEN HALL

◂ Originally laid out by Robert Wynn in the Dutch style, this remarkable garden (which formerly had at its centre a sundial dated 1678) is perfectly set in a deep walled rectangle that allows the full design of the pattern to be viewed with ease from terraces above. The surrounding walls are clothed in yellow Banksian roses *Rosa banksiae* 'Lutea', while china-blue flower spikes of *Echium pininana* appear rather incongruously above the walls.

From the seventeenth century until 1969, Bodysgallen was owned by the Mostyn family and during this period several other gardens were developed. In 1886, Lady Augusta Mostyn created a walled rose garden below the parterre; a lily pool, rock garden and cascade followed in the early years of the twentieth century.

Sadly, from 1949 the garden fell into a period of gradual decline. However, over the past thirty-five years, head gardener Robert Owen and his team have undertaken an award-winning garden restoration. Today, the gardens are a delight and worthy of the acclaim they now receive. New features include avenues of flowering crab apple *Malus floribunda*, drifts of narcissi and other bulbs, plantings of medlar and silver-leaved pear, and a fully functioning productive garden producing fruit and vegetables for the hotel.

◂ Bodysgallen Hall's productive walled garden

Narcissi in the walled garden

BRO MEIGAN

Bro Meigan is an attractive and thoughtfully designed garden situated in beautiful countryside on the northern edge of the Pembrokeshire National Park. From several vantage points and seats, magnificent panoramic vistas can be enjoyed of the Preseli Hills, which are renowned as being the source of the Bluestones found at Stonehenge. In total, it extends to 6.5 acres (2.6 hectares) and is largely made up of a mix of sweeping lawns and colourful shrub and herbaceous borders.

Thirty years ago, Bro Meigan was a smallholding, but the owners at the time saw its potential and began to turn the land into a garden. Following their retirement in 2005, the property was acquired by the present owners. A couple who came to it without any horticultural knowledge but with a great interest in wildlife and the natural world, they have since extensively developed and planted the garden with wildlife in mind. Despite only being managed by the two of them, Bro Meigan has been recognised as one of the best privately run gardens in Wales.

It also includes a beautiful organic wild meadow, a wooded dingle with natural springs and a bog garden all planted and managed to complement the surrounding landscape. ▸

Sweeping lawns and colourful borders at Bro Meigan

Views to the distant hills from Bro Meigan ▸

◀ A large labyrinth with a centrepiece Bluestone encourages the visitor to contemplate the bounty of Mother Nature. What comes through in this garden is that the couple who live here have a deep understanding and love of the environment. Many features, plants and habitats have been incorporated to make the garden as appealing as possible to wildlife, especially birds and insects, including all-important pollinators such as bees, butterflies and hoverflies.

Throughout the garden there is also a huge range of plants that have been deliberately chosen to provide perfume, colour and interest, whatever the season. Many specimen trees have been planted, which have not only improved the structure of the garden but give an ever-changing colour palette throughout the year.

In the surrounding hedgerows, native trees and wild flowers are allowed to grow freely for their fruits, berries and seeds, and provide a haven for nesting birds. This all contributes to the feeling that Bro Meigan is in tune with nature, sympathetic to the natural environment within which it sits and is a peaceful, tranquil location where it is easy to relax and unwind. This is truly a garden that will appeal to gardeners, artists, photographers, birdwatchers and wildlife enthusiasts alike.

Bro Meigan House with Himalayan Birch trees

BRYNGWYN HALL

It is probably fair to say that Bryngwyn Hall, home of the Marchioness of Linlithgow, is not one of the best-known gardens in Wales, but do not read anything into this because it really is a special place and deserves to have a much higher profile than it does. One of the reasons Bryngwyn seems to slip under the radar may be due to the fact that, up until now, access to the garden has only been for pre-booked groups.

Located just north of Welshpool, Bryngwyn is not far from Powis Castle, which is ironically one of the National Trust's most famous gardens. Choosing to visit both in the same day would combine a tried and tested favourite with a hidden garden gem.

Bryngwyn's Grade II listed 9-acre (3.6-hectare) garden wraps around the house and melts seamlessly into a further 60 acres (24 hectares) of oak-studded parkland, designed and laid out by landscape designer William Emes (1730–1803) in the late eighteenth century.

Within the garden many interesting mature trees and shrubs remain from the nineteenth century plantings of Major General Arthur Sandbach, grandfather of Lady Linlithgow, who brought plants, including several fine species of rhododendrons, back from Bhutan, Sikkim and northern India. ▸

A dahlia border at Bryngwyn Hall

◂ The original garden was enlarged in the early twentieth century to encompass a section of the parkland that included one of the park lakes. This became one of the main features visible from the garden. Mown paths were added to cross the sloping lawns that fell away towards a ha-ha and the water beyond, where a slate bench was positioned upon a causeway.

From the 1930s onwards, both house and garden fell into disrepair and remained neglected until Lady Linlithgow began a programme of restoration in 1989. Since then, new yew hedges have been established throughout the garden. These provide structure, foil and protection for an intimate rose garden, and several attractive herbaceous borders packed with new plantings deliberately chosen for their heady summer fragrances and colours as well as further botanical interest.

Spring is well represented at Bryngwyn by drifts of snowdrops and daffodils, which are quickly followed by flowering displays of camellias, rhododendrons and azaleas. In October and early November, spectacular leaf colours emerge from comprehensive collections of maples, cherries and birch, thereby ensuring that autumn is also a good time to visit.

In 2014, a unique 'poison garden' was designed and planted with some of the most poisonous plants in the UK, including Aconitum, Oleander, Hemlock and Ricin.

◂ Cosmos and nicotiana at Bryngwyn Hall

Japanese Maples at Bryngwyn Hall

CAE HIR GARDENS

Begun thirty years ago and opened to the public in 1989, Cae Hir gardens were entirely envisaged, designed and created by just one man, Dutchman Wil Akkermans. Horticulture had been in the Akkermans' blood for generations; Wil's ancestor Johannus Akkermans first set up a nursery near the Dutch town of Breda in the early nineteenth century.

Wil and his wife Gill moved to Cae Hir from the Netherlands in 1983. They had married in 1974, having met in Aberystwyth, where Wil was on holiday. After marrying, they lived in the Netherlands for nine years until Wil decided to follow his dream and create his own garden, which he eventually hoped to open to the public.

Since 1989, Cae Hir has matured into one of Wales' most acclaimed gardens and one that became a partner garden to The Royal Horticultural Society in 2004. Wil passed Cae Hir to his son and daughter Stuart and Julie in 2009, who, while continuing Wil's ethos, are also putting their own stamp on this inspirational garden set within the beautiful West Wales countryside.

Unlike so many gardens, Cae Hir (Welsh for 'long field') has never had the benefit of external funding, grants or donations. ▸

Magnolias and aquilegia at Cae Hir

Ornamental trees, including laburnum and birch ▸

◀ This has been entirely a family venture and it is a real testament to all the Akkermans that they have created a garden that stands up well to just about any other in Wales.

Its strength and originality are founded upon a bold design and a rather unconventional approach to gardening, the overriding criteria being a sympathetic fit with the Welsh countryside and a harmonious blend of native and exotic plants, the wild and the cultivated.

Cae Hir covers 6 acres (2.5 hectares), four on one side of a road and two on the other. The terrain slopes, gently at first, then more steeply, from a summerhouse with far-reaching views across the surrounding countryside down past a natural stream to a series of informal wildlife pools at the bottom. Near the top is a 60-foot-long (18-metre) laburnum crescent underplanted with *Rosa rugosa* and edged with rock cranesbill *Geranium macrorrhizum*.

Clipped yew hedging echoes the crescent shape, before leading to a series of garden rooms separated by serpentine swathes of grass bespotted with ornamental trees, such as *Betula albosinensis*, and fringed with perennials. Each room has a different theme, be it colour, plants or style. Topiary, bonsai and wild flowers add to the mix in this beautifully designed but informal garden landscape.

Sweeping lawns and foxgloves

CAERAU UCHAF GARDENS

Situated over 1,000 ft (304 m) above sea level, with far reaching views over the Berwyn Mountains, Bala Lake and Cadair Idris, the gardens at Caerau are believed to be the highest gardens open to the public in Wales. While this might be an interesting fact to use when promoting the garden, it does lead one to question whether in such a challenging environment it is possible to establish a garden that has real horticultural merit. Well, the simple answer is yes. What Toby and Stephanie Hickish have managed to achieve since they first moved to the property in 1994 is quite remarkable. Back then, Caerau Uchaf was a derelict house and the garden no more than a field. While planning permission was sought to renovate and restore the house, Toby and Stephanie started work on creating a garden.

They were not coming to this as novices; between them they ran award-winning garden design, landscaping and garden maintenance companies, which, over the years, have been responsible for many show gardens at prestigious events such as the RHS shows at Hampton Court and Tatton Park. Also, for a period, Toby worked with the Welsh gardening programme Clwb Garddio and was responsible for designing and building all the themed gardens at Rhostryfan, the home of the programme. ▶

The cottage and gardens at Caerau Uchaf

◂ As a result of their work, they were able to salvage plants and structures after these events, which they could adapt for use in their own gardens at Caerau Uchaf. Consequently, the gardens have evolved quite quickly and remarkably show little sign of their traumatic move from cosseted Hampton Court Palace grounds to North Wales mountainside. Of course, plenty has been done to lessen the exposure of the site by the strategic planting of shelterbelts of trees, but even these have needed to become established before they could offer meaningful shelter to other plants.

Caerau gardens were not designed with the idea of opening to the public, so there is not a set route around them. It is a series of different areas with paths linking and hedges dividing. However, as a visitor, this makes for a fascinating experience, as you are never quite sure what lies around the corner. There are crescent-shaped herbaceous borders, laburnum-covered pergolas, rose gardens, castellated yew topiary, an arboretum containing some fine Japanese maples, pleached lime walkways, courtyard gardens, a variegated ivy-clad water feature and even a beach hut! Not only that, there is also an excellent café serving homemade meals and cakes.

◂ Gardens with far-reaching views

A beach hut at Caerau Uchaf

❈ CENTRE FOR ALTERNATIVE TECHNOLOGY

The Centre for Alternative Technology (CAT) is situated high in a former slate quarry, surrounded by glorious countryside, on the edge of Coed y Brenin Forest Park.

Founded in the mid-1970s, by a group of environmentally friendly individuals who wanted to create a sustainable community, CAT was once thought of as the place where 'well-meaning hippies went to put the world to rights'. Well, over the past forty years, their environmental views have not changed, but the views of the rest of the world have. No longer seen as 'slightly quirky', the work carried out at CAT is now very much at the centre of government thinking and policy, and their pioneering ideas have filtered through to all of us in a multitude of ways from recycling and organics to renewable energy and environmental architecture.

At the heart of this 7-acre (2.8-hectare) site is one of the most exciting horticultural projects in Wales, including a whole series of display gardens from which we can take ideas away to use in our own gardens. Yes, we have all read books and articles on environmentally sustainable gardening, but actually seeing it in action is so much more helpful. ▸

◂ Hydrangeas across the lawn at Caerau Uchaf

The Forest Garden at the Centre for Alternative Technology

◀ In the 'Whole Home Garden', a suburban -sized garden shows how to have a productive and wildlife-friendly garden, and includes planting for beneficial insects, composting, organic herbs and flower borders, an environmentally managed lawn, organically grown fruit, heritage vegetables and seed saving. The 'Urban Garden' shows that even in the very centre of a city, with virtually no garden or soil, a range of tasty, fresh vegetables, fruit and herbs can be grown.

There are displays on how to get the best out of your greenhouse or polytunnel all year round using a whole range of plants including figs, grapes, peaches, squashes, peppers and salads – much of which makes its way into the excellent organic café on site. 'The Mole Hole' provides a fascinating insight into how to keep beneficial creatures in our soil happy and healthy, and a whole range of green manure beds provides examples of plants you can grow to improve your garden fertility. Mulching, lawn feeds, allotment management, increasing pollinators and organic pest and disease controls are also tackled, as are how to use natural and recycled materials to form harmoniously shaped raised beds, ponds, sheds and garden sculpture.

Do not expect this garden to be to RHS standards of tidiness and regimentation, but maybe, just maybe, that's the point.

◀ Pioneering ideas on renewable energy in the garden

Teaching organic gardening

CHIRK CASTLE

Located in a commanding position high above the Welsh borderlands, Chirk Castle is said to have views that encompass fourteen Welsh and English counties. Completed in 1300, it is one of Edward I's formidable 'chain of castles' built with the express intention of subduing the Welsh. No longer a military stronghold, for much of the past 400 years Chirk Castle was home to the Myddelton family and it was during their tenure that the land around this medieval fortress evolved into an intriguing mix of formal and informal gardens. Today, the National Trust works hard to conserve the historical nature of the landscape, while at the same time maintaining and developing a garden fit for the twenty-first century and beyond.

Original paths, a bowling green and summerhouses were lost when landscape designer William Emes laid down the bones of the present parkland, complete with its majestic oaks and sweet chestnuts, in 1764. After the Second World War, 6 acres (2.5 hectares) of ornamental gardens were planted by Lady Margaret Myddleton. Today they include many unusual rhododendrons and azaleas, the flowers of which light up the spring landscape with vibrant clouds of colour. Here too are magnolias, camellias, pieris, Chilean lantern trees *Crinodendron hookerianum*, fire bushes *Embothrium coccineum*, delicate bell-flowered *Enkianthus campanulatus* and a fine handkerchief tree *Davidia involucrata*, which only sheds its flamboyant cream-white bracts once the first dogwood flowers appear on a nearby *Cornus kousa*. ▸

Chirk Castle and topiary

Chirk Castle ornamental garden ▸

◀ From Lady Myddleton's ornamental garden, an avenue of lime trees, fringed by drifts of narcissi, leads to a statue of Hercules, where fine vistas open up towards the castle and its accompanying formal garden. Here, scores of yew trees, planted in the late nineteenth century, have been shaped into glorious domes and 'Welsh hats' on a scale that rivals the topiary at Levens Hall in Cumbria. Along with a series of long, crenellated hedges, carefully crafted to mimic the stone defences of the castle, they provide work for three National Trust gardeners, who take from August to October each year to clip the yews back into shape. Enclosed within the topiary is a rose garden, which provides both summer fragrance and colour. There is also a 900-foot-long (275-metre) meandering herbaceous border, which is planted in four bays representing the four seasons, and a thatched Hawk House, covered by ornamental vines and *Eccremocarpus scaber*, and flanked by a sloping rock bank overflowing with choice shrubs and ferns.

The thatched hawk house at Chirk Castle

CLYNE GARDENS

Owned and managed today by Swansea City Council, Clyne was once the home of the wealthy nineteenth-century Vivian family. The house, originally built in 1791, was purchased along with the surrounding estate by millionaire William Graham Vivian in 1860. He lavished time and money on it, turning it into a Victorian Gothic 'castle' in the process. Around the 'castle', he developed woodland gardens and sweeping parkland dotted with clumps of trees, using a mix of British natives such as oak and beech, and exotic newcomers including North American giant redwoods *Sequoiadendron giganteum* and Monterey Cypress *Cupressus macrocarpa* – one of which is now the tallest of its kind in Wales. If you are a tree lover, this is the place for you; Clyne has a remarkable arboreal collection including one of the largest magnolias in Britain, *Magnolia campbellii* Alba Group.

In 1921, the Clyne estate passed to William Vivian's nephew, Admiral Algernon, who owned it until his death in 1952 when it eventually came into the hands of Swansea City Council. It was Algernon who had the greatest influence on the 50-acre (20-hectare) Grade I Welsh Historic Garden that exists today. He was a keen amateur botanist and plantsman, and sponsored several plant collecting expeditions overseas. ▸

Clyne bog garden (*Image courtesy of Alan Gregg*)

◂ A good proportion of the plants that exist at Clyne today can be directly attributed to him, including many of Clyne's rhododendrons, some of which still bear their original collector's numbers. The Admiral's influence can also be seen in some of Clyne's landscape features including a Japanese-style bridge, Gazebo and the Admiral's Tower, built so that he could survey his plant collection from above.

Clyne boasts three National Collections (Plant Heritage), pieris, enkianthus and rhododendron (Triflora and Falconera subsections). Consequently, the most interesting time to visit is undoubtedly the spring, when the enormous collection of rhododendrons (over 800 varieties, some of them very rare) are at their best, including several hybrids raised by Admiral Algernon such as *Rhododendron niveum* 'Clyne Castle' and 'Singleton Blue'. These are mostly found on the banks above the stream that runs through the garden and makes for a glorious walk, ending up at the Japanese-style-bridge. Clyne's bog garden is also situated in this area with extensive plantings of *Gunnera manicata*, candelabra primula, *Iris pseudacorus* and other self-spreading species, including meadowsweet and, later in the year, crocosmia. In May there will also be swathes of bluebells and wild garlic in the woodland areas.

◂ **Bananas and crocosmia at Clyne Gardens** *(Image courtesy of Alan Gregg)*

The woodland garden with rhododendrons

❁ CONWY VALLEY MAZE

Perhaps one of the lesser-known gardens in Wales, but also one of the most intriguing, is the Conwy Valley Maze Garden, just a stone's throw from Bodnant on the eastern edge of the Snowdonia National Park. It is situated in a glorious location with views of surrounding mountains, their lower slopes verdantly clothed in the plantations of Gwydyr Forest.

The maze, which extends to over 2 acres (1 hectare), is said to be the largest garden maze in the world and was created in 2005 by garden owner Giovanni Angelo Jacovelli with help from renowned Australian artist Bob Haberfield. It sits within a further 8 acres (3.2 hectares), which includes woodland walks, waterfalls, art installations and sculpture.

As might be expected, the maze is created using close-clipped yew *Taxus baccata* – over 2,500 of them.

Nothing unusual in that you might say. However, what makes this maze unique is the fact that it contains several themed gardens that can only be accessed by following the correct paths through the maze. Each garden is effectively your prize for successfully negotiating your way through sections of the maze. Within this evergreen labyrinth, there is a rose garden containing over 200 roses and a pergola archway, which is on a similar scale to the laburnum arch at Bodnant. Further into the maze, a subtropical garden is revealed, full of tender plants that excel in this temperate corner of North Wales, and, finally, the ultimate prize, a Japanese-style Zen Buddhist garden, which, with a little imagination, transports you to the Ginkakuji Temple Garden in Kyoto, Japan. ▸

Conwy Valley Maze from above

Sculptures and statues adorn the maze ▸

◂ Here, stone lanterns, perfectly placed rocks and a sea of raked silver-white gravel are visually held together by the careful planting of evergreen azaleas, Japanese acers and cloud-clipped yew topiary.

So, what took Giovanni down this unusual garden route in the first place? Well, a teenage memory of visiting Compton Acres left him with a desire to employ the technique of compartmentalising garden spaces, and what better way to do this than within a maze? Never having previously been in a maze, he set about designing a layout, based around differing gardens, along with lengthy vistas. The result is both unusual and inspirational, and has the ability to appeal to all, be they serious gardeners or young families with children. Now that is important; those young people may well turn into tomorrow's serious gardeners.

The rose garden at Conwy Valley Maze

COWBRIDGE PHYSIC GARDEN

Cowbridge Physic Garden is located 12 miles west of Cardiff in the small South Wales town of Cowbridge. It is positioned within the grounds of Cowbridge Old Hall, the eighteenth-century home of the Edmondes family, and bordered on its south side by medieval town walls. Despite its proximity to the centre of town, once inside, the garden breathes the very essence of peace and tranquillity.

There is some suggestion that there has been a garden on this site since the seventeenth century; records show that in the nineteenth century this area was laid out with regular beds and paths in a way not dissimilar to that found in the half-acre (0.2-hectare) Physic Garden today. After the departure of the Edmondes family from Old Hall in the 1920s, the site became first a kitchen garden for nearby Cowbridge Grammar School and then a tree nursery for the local authority. However, by the final years of the twentieth century, the land had been neglected for some time and was an overgrown wilderness.

In 2004, a group of volunteers keen to re-establish horticulture on the site set up the Cowbridge Physic Garden Charitable Trust. Clearance of the site began in early 2005. ▸

The entrance to Cowbridge Physic Garden

◂ The plan was to create a formal design not only echoing the original garden layout, but also reflecting the style of physic gardens that abounded in Britain in the seventeenth century. Construction of the garden began in August 2005 and was completed a year later, with volunteers toiling a further two years to plant the garden. It was officially opened by Her Royal Highness the Duchess of Cornwall in June 2008.

Today, Cowbridge Physic Garden displays a range of plants found in Britain before 1800, all of which have in one way or another been helpful to man. The collection includes plants used in medicine, in the kitchen, for perfume and cosmetics and for dyeing fabrics. However, this is not purely a functional garden; it has been laid out in a way that is both aesthetically appealing and relaxing.

Areas around the perimeter of the garden emphasise colour and fragrance, and include fruit grown either as espalier or over pergolas. The twelve main beds at the core of the garden surround a central pool and fountain, and are devoted to medicinal plants. Each bed contains plants specific to a part of the body or a particular illness. Individual plants may ease an ailment, but collectively this garden is good for the soul.

◂ Espalier fruit at Cowbridge Physic Garden

Medlar and bay trees

CRUG FARM PLANTS

Perched on an exposed hillside near Caernarfon and little more than a stone's throw from the Menai Strait is one of the most exciting plant collections in Wales. Crug (pronounced 'Creeg') Farm is the home of Bleddyn and Sue Wynn-Jones, former fashion buyer and farmer turned expert plant collectors. Since 1991, they have taken part in over sixty plant-hunting expeditions overseas in search of new and exotic plants to introduce into their 20-acre (8-hectare) garden and plant nursery.

Crug Farm is a magnet for anyone who has the slightest interest in growing something different to the bulk standard menu found in the majority of garden centres. Not only that, it is the place to go to listen and learn as Bleddyn imparts fascinating advice on where and how to grow these botanical curiosities. In truth, his botanical knowledge is superb, which is not bad considering that for much of his early working life he was a beef farmer and strawberry grower.

Crug is made up of three separate gardens, all small but crammed with specimens collected from Bleddyn and Sue's plant hunting expeditions across the world – China, Vietnam, Costa Rica, Taiwan, Mexico and The Azores are just some of the countries represented here. ▸

The walled enclosure at Crug Farm

Polyspora longicarpa ▸

◂ Yet despite this exotic and potentially tender cornucopia of flora, nothing is grown under glass. Everything has to be able to survive outside in a garden where wind speeds can reach 100 mph (160 km/h) and temperatures have been known to fall below minus 10 degrees centigrade. According to Bleddyn, there are two reasons for this: firstly, they only collect plants from high altitude, which means they are likely to be used to frost and snow; secondly, each plant is given optimum shelter. Surrounding the garden are shelter-belts of evergreen and deciduous trees and shrubs, and, at the very centre, a walled enclosure houses the more tender specimens such as *Pittosporum illicioides* from Taiwan and the beautiful camellia-like *Polyspora longicarpa* from Vietnam.

Seed collected overseas is first germinated in a series of polytunnels and then plants are tested for hardiness in nursery beds, before making it into the garden and then eventually to the plant sales area, which is itself a delight, surrounded by white-walled potting sheds and trellis smothered by Schizophragma and Holboellia. Do not expect manicured lawns and cleverly executed vistas in this garden – the whole experience is all about the plants, which collectively would make any botanic garden in the world proud.

Rare plant sales at Crug Farm

DEWSTOW

Situated in the Monmouthshire countryside, just a few miles from the M4 and the two River Severn crossings, Dewstow is a 'lost garden' that was regarded during the lifetime of its Victorian creator, Henry 'Squire' Oakley, as 'a unique and wondrous local landmark'. Most wondrous of all was the extensive labyrinth of underground manmade tunnels containing fern-filled caverns, tufa grottoes, artificial stalagmites, pools and fountains, all of which were buried under thousands of tons of soil for over fifty years.

Originally built around 1895 by James Pulham and Son, who were one of the most respected landscape gardening companies of the late nineteenth and early twentieth centuries, the gardens and grottoes were deliberately buried just after the Second World War and only rediscovered when new owners took over the property in 2000. Soon after, a large-scale excavation and restoration operation swung into action. In time, this revealed that although some areas were in very poor condition, other tunnels and grottoes remained almost as good as the day they were constructed.

Today, most of the restoration work is complete, and the garden, which in total covers 7 acres (2.8 hectares), is now fully open to the public. ▸

One of Dewstow's many pools

◂ Not all of this area is underground; the tunnels and grottoes, which were originally made of a mixture of real stone and faced stone using several different types of Pulhamite, account for approximately one third of the area, and the rest is laid to meandering lawns, island beds, herbaceous borders and a delightful ravine garden containing a series of bog gardens, lakes and small waterfalls all interconnected by a meandering stream.

It is, however, below ground that you will most probably spend the larger proportion of your time. Here in this fascinating subterranean world, lit by a combination of natural light filtering though glazed skylights in the cavern roofs and artificial electric light, is a garden environment seldom seen in Britain, and one that in a small way is slightly reminiscent of the volcanic lava tube caverns, worked into glorious gardens by Cesar Manrique, at Jameos del Agua on the Canary Island of Lanzarote.

At Dewstow, most pleasing of all is the Lion Grotto. Here the warm, frost-free, shaded and humid atmosphere is perfect for tropical rainforest palms, arums, orchids, begonias, climbing fig *Ficus pumila* and flowering succulents. A short tunnel walk away is the fern grotto, which features tropical and subtropical ferns from all over the world including roof-high Australasian tree ferns.

◂ The Lion Grotto

Dewstow Tropical Oasis

❁ DINGLE GARDEN

Hidden in a quiet, secluded valley just a couple of miles north of the market town of Welshpool lies the Dingle Garden, a stunning 4-acre (1.6-hectare) botanical oasis set amid the gloriously wild sheep-lands of Mid Wales. Created in the main by Barbara (Barbie) Joseph and her husband Roy over a period lasting some thirty-five years, from 1968 until 2003, this really is a perfect example of that much overused phrase 'a garden for all seasons'.

Dingle's garden year begins when the cool valley air becomes delicately scented by late-flowering sarcococcas and early-flowering daphnes. As temperatures rise, blooms from hundreds of different shrubs, including rhododendrons, azaleas, pieris and camellias, flood the valley with light and colour, which is complemented by swathes of primroses and bluebells in the surrounding woodland. Summer brings the semi-formal layout of the lawn garden to the fore, where clever and dramatic use of herbaceous plantings in serpentine beds is set against the sun terrace of an adjacent cottage. As daylight hours lessen, the sweet caramel-like fragrance of several Katsura trees *Cercidiphyllum japonicum* herald the arrival of autumn, which is perhaps one of the finest times of year to visit Dingle. ▸

The lower lake at Dingle

Slopes covered with ornamental trees and shrubs ▸

◂ It is then that fiery leaf colours of acers, nyssas and liquidambars take centre stage, each tree doubled in its effectiveness by reflections upon the mirror-like surfaces of two lakes in the valley bottom. Even in winter the drama is maintained; barks of Chinese paper-bark maples, Tibetan cherries and Australasian snow gums positively glow against a backdrop of evergreens.

Although not particularly large, this garden feels much bigger than it actually is, and this is due to several factors: firstly, the topography, which brings the benefit of hills and slopes that can be used to effectively display plants in a way that allows them to be viewed both from above and below; secondly, water, which offers stillness and reflections upon the two lake surfaces and then movement and sound from the inter-connecting stream; finally, the garden is cleverly designed around a series of meandering paths, which offer up teases and unexpected 'reveals' at every twist and turn.

It would be remiss not to mention the excellent nursery that sits alongside the entrance to the garden and offers a superb selection of plants for sale, ranging from seedlings and herbaceous plants to shrubs and trees. Inspiration for the nursery comes from the garden, which in turn provides a 'shop window' for you to choose from.

Australian snow gums

DYFFRYN GARDENS AND ARBORETUM

This remarkable 55-acre (22-hectare) Grade I listed Edwardian garden, located in the heart of the Vale of Glamorgan, has as its centre a grandiose Grade II listed mansion remodelled in 1893 for coal magnate John Cory, who had purchased the property two years earlier. Cory commissioned eminent landscape architect Thomas Mawson to design a garden around the house and a master plan was produced in 1903/04, although work did not begin in earnest until 1906. After John Cory's death in 1910, his son, Reginald, who had studied Law at Cambridge but found horticulture much more interesting, collaborated with Mawson on the design and over time became a fine horticulturalist and enthusiastic plant collector, sponsoring expeditions for plant hunters such as George Forrest, Ernest Wilson and Harold Coomber.

Members of the Cory family continued to live at Dyffryn until 1936, and, shortly afterwards the property was leased to Glamorgan County Council and eventually purchased by Vale of Glamorgan Council, who, with the help of a Heritage Lottery Fund grant, began a process of restoration to both house and garden. In 2013, the National Trust took over stewardship of Dyffryn on a fifty-year lease and is continuing with that work. ▸

Dyffryn House and bedding scheme

◂ In their original and somewhat eclectic design, Mawson and Reginald Cory managed to incorporate features and styles from several periods in British garden history as well as influences from around the world. Nowhere is this more obvious than in the Roman-styled Pompeian Garden, inspired by their joint visit to Italy in 1908. Here columns, colonnades, fountains and loggias are softened by wisteria and clematis. Other themed outdoor garden 'rooms' include a Mediterranean Garden, Physic Garden, Theatre Garden (where Cory displayed his collection of Bonsai), Cloisters, Reflecting Pool Garden, Rose Garden and Lavender Court. In some ways these 'rooms' were ahead of their time, as they predate those at Hidcote Manor and Sissinghurst by several years.

Linking everything together is a much larger landscape, befitting such a grand house, with lawns, borders, topiary, an extensive arboretum of rare trees, a very fine rock garden set upon a natural limestone outcrop, a heather garden and a central canal running southwards from the house. Some of the finest restoration work to date includes gloriously colourful herbaceous borders, a productive Walled Garden full of vegetables, fruit and cut flowers, and a Glass House that contains excellent displays of orchids and cacti. Give the day over to this garden – it deserves it.

◂ Herbaceous borders at Dyffryn

Dyffryn Pompeian Italian garden

ERDDIG

Historic Erddig is a rare surviving example of early eighteenth-century formal garden design in the Dutch style. Prior to the 1970s, parts of this Grade I historic garden were lost beneath a rampant blanket of woody weeds, brambles and trees. However, in March 1973, Philip Yorke passed the 2,000-acre (809-hectare) estate and house, which had been his family's ancestral home for almost 250 years, to the National Trust and they began a sympathetic and thoughtful restoration. At the time it was the largest garden restoration the National Trust had ever undertaken and they were guided by a garden plan drawn by Thomas Badeslade in 1739.

Today, Erddig's 13-acre (5.2-hectare) garden restoration is complete. Gravelled walkways cut crisply through close-mown turf planted with lines of pleached limes *Tilia x euchlora*, shaped Portuguese laurel *Prunus lusitanica* growing in white-painted planters, variegated hollies and Irish yew cones. There is also a broad canal and pool, which would have originally been stocked with fish for the table. Orchards located near the garden entrance and directly in front of the house, contain varieties of fruit known (from a surviving inventory) to have been grown here in 1718. They include pears such as Bon-Chrétien d'Hiver, Red Magnum Bonum plums and Fenouillet Rouge apples. ▸

A formal garden in the Dutch style

Wall fruit in the gardener's yard ▸

◂ In all, there are over 180 different varieties of fruit at Erddig, growing as espaliers, in orchards and in regimental patterns across the lawns, where the formality is softened by swathes of narcissus, lent lily, pheasant's eye and fritillaries. There is also a National Collection of ivies *Hedera sp.*, members of which can be seen growing on the red-brick walls throughout the property.

Although the early eighteenth-century garden is all about structure and formality, the Yorke family continued to develop and add ornamental features to the garden throughout the nineteenth century. South of the Canal Walk is the Victorian Flower Garden, where climbing roses and clematis clamber along looping swags above colourful bulbs and herbaceous plantings. Other Victorian additions include a parterre with lichen-covered fountain, further rose gardens, ornamental trees, and shrubs and beds planted with colourful annuals fashionable when the British Empire was at its height.

Beyond the garden to the west are views across woodland and parkland laid out by William Emes in the 1770s, and a short walk from the house reveals the unusual 'Cup and Saucer' weir – a circular pool with nearby hydraulic ram pump, originally installed to raise water for the house.

Pleached lime trees at Erddig

GLANSEVERN HALL GARDENS

Glansevern Hall was built in the Greek revival style between 1801 and 1806 by Arthur Davies Owen, and is romantically positioned alongside the River Severn in beautiful parkland with far-reaching views across the Mid-Wales countryside. Immediately surrounding the hall is a 25-acre (10-hectare) Welsh Historic Grade ll Listed garden, which has been sympathetically restored and re-established over the past thirty-five years.

The garden includes sweeping lawns, island beds brimming with herbaceous plants and a 4-acre (1.6-hectare) lake complete with resident waterfowl. Paths meander around the lake passing unusual ornamental trees that have been underplanted with flowering shrubs and bulbs deliberately chosen to provide colour and interest throughout the year. At the far end of the lake is a delightful water garden with streams and cascade all fed from the nearby Montgomeryshire Canal, and planted with a selection of moisture-loving plants including candelabra primulas and hostas.

The main garden is accessed from the visitor entrance, tea room and gallery shop via a pair of magnificent metal gates. These carry scrolls and whorls inspired by the primeval-shaped leaves of the Ginkgo tree, which are akin in outline to the maidenhair fern. ▶

Gingko Gates

❋ GLANSEVERN HALL GARDENS

◂ Beyond the gates lies the walled garden. Originally built in 1805, it was completely restored in 2001 by then-owners Neville and Jenny Thomas, who had purchased Glansevern in 1982 at a time when much of the estate and hall had fallen into disrepair. They worked hard to restore the hall and all of Glansevern's gardens to their former glory, first opening the gardens to the public in 1996. Although now retired, they continue to offer invaluable advice to the present owner.

Today, the walled garden is subdivided into a series of separate garden 'rooms', which include a rose garden, a white garden, a kitchen and a cutting garden. In late summer, the borders full of dahlias and chrysanthemums are particularly colourful. The use of climbers throughout the walled garden is inspiring, particularly along the main axis pergola walkway, which is draped with *Akebia quinata*, and in the fruit garden, where espaliered apples and pears are intertwined with several different varieties of clematis. Beyond the walled garden is a huge Victorian rock garden and grotto dating from around 1840, a wisteria walk that leads to a fountain, a recently created rill garden and a south-facing orangery dating from 1830, containing citrus trees, the Brazilian glory bush *Tibouchina urvilleana* and several fine specimens of angel's trumpets *Brugmansia x candida*.

◂ Glansevern Dahlia collection Glansevern Orangery

GLYNLLIFON

The Glynllifon estate is located on a site that is documented as having been in human occupation for almost 1,000 years. This is perhaps unsurprising given its close proximity to the strategically important town and port of Caernarfon, which stands guard over the westerly approaches to Anglesey and the Menai Strait. The Roman fort of Segontium lies just a few miles away to the north.

At the centre of the estate is Plas Glynllifon, a stunning building constructed between 1836 and 1849, which is considered to be one of the finest Regency-style mansions in North Wales. It was originally the seat of the Lords Newborough and remained with the family from the eighteenth century until 1948 when much of the estate was sold off. Since then the mansion has had a somewhat chequered history. It was the location for HRH the Prince of Wales' Investiture Ball in 1969, but latterly has suffered periods of neglect interspersed with partial renovation, restoration and management by various owners and bodies, including hoteliers.

Despite this, the surrounding 700-acre (283-hectare) estate, which is part run as a land-based educational facility and part managed by Gwynedd County Council, is a fascinating location. ▸

Glynllifon Amphitheatre

Glynllifon Boat House ▸

◀ It includes a Grade I Listed landscaped park (parc), which is also designated as an SSSI (Site of Special Scientific Interest) due to the fact that there are rare examples of local flora and fauna here, including several endangered ferns and lesser horseshoe bats.

Glynllifon's landscaped parc and gardens were initially laid out in the late eighteenth and early nineteenth centuries in typical picturesque landscape style, and include fine vistas towards the northerly section of the Snowdon mountain massif. Flowing through the length of the parc is the Afon Llifon, which in the past has been enhanced and aesthetically improved by the introduction of water cascades, bridges and basins. Growing alongside and throughout the woodland are ancient ornamental flowering shrubs, including rhododendrons, while in spring the lawns in front of the mansion come alive with drifts of narcissi.

When visiting Glynllifon, do not expect to see regularly pruned plants, well maintained pathways and perfect signage; today, this is a neglected landscape and one that is crying out for care, funding and restoration. Until that happens, think *The Secret Garden* and enjoy walking beneath its giant American redwoods and Chilean pines, while savouring the enchanting atmosphere that surrounds its crumbling, moss-covered and lichen encrusted amphitheatre, fountains, ponds, boathouse, grottoes and hermit's cave.

Glynllifon Cascade

GREGYNOG

Gregynog Hall lies in an attractive hidden valley just north of Newtown in the old Welsh county of Montgomeryshire. It is surrounded by 750 acres (303 hectares) of Grade I listed gardens and grounds. Described by CADW as 'one of the most important parks and gardens in Powys', it is in part the creation of eighteenth-century landscape designer William Emes.

Gregynog is approached along a winding drive bordered by exotic conifers of immense proportions and billowing clouds of Victorian-planted rhododendrons. The considerable length of the drive gradually but firmly establishes the feeling that you are about to arrive somewhere special, yet nothing quite prepares you for the first glimpse of the hall. It resembles an enormous black-and-white timber-framed Elizabethan farmhouse, but few such buildings ever attained these proportions. A closer look destroys the illusion. The façade of Gregynog is not timber, but concrete. The building could be considered to be a fake, a wealthy nineteenth-century industrialist's take on a fantasy Elizabethan mansion. However, behind the concrete is a very old house indeed and one established on a settlement dating back to the twelfth century.

The current 1860 façade was the initiative of Gregynog owners the Hanbury-Tracy family, newly rich ironmasters from Pontypool and pioneers in the use of concrete as a building material. ▸

The concrete façade of Gregynog Hall

◂ As well as enlarging and encasing the house in concrete, they created concrete bridges, pools and fountains within the gardens – gardens which by 1894 were considered among the finest within mid-Wales.

The wealth of the Hanbury-Tracys was short-lived and, by the First World War, much of the 18,000-acre (7,284-hectare) estate had been sold off. The hall, gardens and immediate grounds were purchased by the Davies family, who have been described as 'a family with money and a social conscience'. During their tenure, Gregynog became the centre for the arts, including painting, music, printing, pottery, weaving and furniture making. In the 1950s, Gregynog was given to the University of Wales, who have endeavoured to keep that same spirit alive.

The gardens are still beautiful, even though there are only three gardeners compared to twenty-six prior to 1914! Rhododendrons and azaleas abound and uniquely shaped close-clipped yew hedging, herbaceous borders and rose gardens provide worthy accompaniment to the hall.

In the wider landscape, beech trees rise above lakes and water gardens, ancient oak woodland is designated a Site of Special Scientific Interest (SSSI) and, directly opposite the hall, a magnificent collection of trees dates back to the 1880s.

◂ A giant redwood tree and a giant hand

Gregynog Hall with topiary hedge

GWYDIR CASTLE

Few gardens in Wales can match the atmosphere and romanticism of Gwydir Castle. From the moment of arrival, the echoing call of peacocks resonating among the surrounding spruce trees of Gwydyr Forest welcomes you to a bygone age. Once through the heavy oak gates, you enter a world that is seldom encountered in the fast-moving twenty-first century.

In some ways, this is hardly surprising given that the garden surrounds a beautiful building dating back to the sixteenth century and stands on the site of an earlier fourteenth-century manorial house.

However, all of us have visited old castles before and remained untouched due to restoration 'improvements', health and safety accommodations and overzealous interpretation – not so Gwydir. Here past centuries rush forward to greet you, offering up mustiness, tread-worn stonework, creakingly communicative smoke-stained timbers and a constant neck-tingling awareness of past generations.

All of this would suggest that no modern-day hand is at play here, whereas, in fact, a sensitive and sympathetic restoration of the castle has been ongoing since Judy Corbett and Peter Welford acquired the property in 1994. ▸

Gwydir Castle and Knot Garden

Yew topiary cones flank the entrance to the Knot Garden ▸

All of this is exquisitely documented within Judy's bestselling book *Castles in the Air*, published in 2004. More than a decade later the work is still continuing, but you would be hard pushed to say exactly what and where and the garden is described as 'a journey in progress'. However, this is the point – it will always be in progress because there is no final destination, just a gentle guiding hand ensuring that if previous visitors, such as King Charles I, returned for a day, they would have little comprehension that almost four centuries had passed since their previous visit.

Of course the seventeenth-century Lebanon cedars on the main lawns are now multi-limbed, battered and bruised veterans, but the giant 600-year-old yew, known locally as the 'Lovers Tree' would have looked much the same to Charles, and the formal planting and structure to the terracing is comfortably Elizabethan.

To the north-west of the castle, the Old Dutch Garden still has its fountain and some of its ancient yew topiary and where these have gone newly planted holly trees now flank the lawn. In the more intimate spaces to the south-east, Peter and Judy have resisted the temptation to flood the knot garden with colourful modern day cultivars and allowed lady's mantle *Alchemilla mollis* and hardy geraniums to informally fill the gaps between the box borders. Step back in time and enjoy.

An ancient Lebanon cedar

HIGH GLANAU MANOR

Situated high above Monmouth with spectacular westerly views across the Vale of Usk towards the Brecon Beacons, High Glanau is a beautiful Grade II listed Arts and Crafts house and garden designed in 1923 by Henry Avray Tipping in collaboration with local young architect Eric Francis. Tipping had previously purchased the land ready for his retirement, having decided it was the ideal place to create his 'gardener's cottage'.

From 1907 until his death in 1933, Tipping was architectural editor of *Country Life* magazine and a great exponent of the Arts & Crafts Movement, which championed a return to the traditional values, quality craftsmanship and attention to detail practiced in Britain prior to the Industrial Revolution.

At High Glanau and within his other garden commissions, such as Wyndcliffe Court, Tipping used local stone, local oak timber and vernacular architecture to design gardens that were at one with their surroundings. Once the hard landscaping was complete he used sublime drifts of herbaceous plantings and climbing roses to both soften and complement the architecture.

When present owners Hilary and Helena Gerrish first saw the property in 2002, little of the original herbaceous plantings remained, the top of the oak and stone-pillared pergola had fallen down and Tipping's ribbon parterre had been replaced by an outdoor swimming pool. ▶

Herbaceous borders with irises and delphiniums at High Glanau

◂ Helena contacted *Country Life* magazine to ask if there were any old photographs available of the original garden and, to her delight, they supplied twenty-four black-and-white images taken by Tipping himself in 1927. This has since enabled her to successfully restore the garden to Tipping's original 1923 design.

Today, High Glanau is once again a horticultural and architectural delight and one that has recently been featured on BBC TV's *Gardeners' World*. The house itself is set above the garden, which is accessed via two westerly-facing stone-flagged terraces complete with octagonal lily pool fringed with roses. Below the terraces, meandering paths lead beneath rhododendron bowers to a small stream with moisture-loving foliage plants. To the side of the house are magnificent recreations of Tipping's herbaceous borders, fringed by golden *Alchemilla mollis* and contrasting beautifully with blue delphiniums, nepeta and *Iris sibirica*.

With the swimming pool now gone, pergola restored, Edwardian glasshouse and productive garden fully functioning, springtime displays of tulips and other bulbs and a wildflower orchard, there can be little doubt that if Tipping were ever to return to High Glanau he would be very pleased with the work of Hilary and Helena Gerrish.

◂ High Glanau House with garden terrace

Octagonal pool from the terrace

LLANERCHAERON

Set in the beautiful Aeron valley in West Wales, Llanerchaeron, or as it was once known Llanayron House, is a rare surviving example of an eighteenth-century Welsh country gentleman's estate. Positioned close to the Afon Aeron, which flows through the estate and on to the sea at Aberaeron, 3 miles to the south-east, Llanerchaeron has at its heart a Grade I Listed mansion, built by John Nash in 1795 for estate owner Major William Lewis on what is believed to be the site of an earlier mansion.

Now in the care of the National Trust for Wales, what makes Llanerchaeron so unique is the fact that later owners allowed most of the estate, including an extensive range of nineteenth-century farm and horticultural buildings such as potting shed, frameyard, farmyard, rickyard, threshing barn, granary, stableyard, cowshed and walled kitchen gardens to enter a graceful state of decline, with no attempt being made to renovate, modernise or demolish them.

Consequently, Llanerchaeron survived practically intact right through to the twentieth century and now provides a clear picture of what life was like on an eighteenth-century, virtually self-sufficient estate and how essential tasks, such as providing food and drink for the table, would have been carried out. ▸

Llanerchaeron Kitchen Garden

Raised beds with herbs and flowers for cutting ▸

◂ Onsite estate services included a dairy, large laundry, brewery, buttery and cheese-making facilities, salting house and smokery for the preservation of meat and fish, and dry storage for overwintering fruit and vegetables.

Today, the restored walled gardens, which are extensive in size and sit at the very core of the estate, are once again being run as an organic, productive kitchen garden, full of colourful flowers, fragrant herbs, traditional vegetables and soft fruit, much of which is available for sale to visitors. Within the walls, there are two interlinked rectangular gardens with traditional vegetable beds complemented by areas for cutting flowers, a parterre planted with roses and annuals and long herbaceous borders. The whole provides a fascinating insight into the development of gardening techniques and technology from the late eighteenth century to the present day.

Llanerchaeron also boasts many veteran fruit trees, such as apples, pears and plums, some nearly 200 years old, which, in addition to their fruit, provide important habitats for invertebrates, mosses and lichens.

Outside the garden, there are tranquil walks along permissive paths through parkland and pleasure grounds, which include an ornamental lake and Home Farm land where Welsh Black cattle, Llanwenog sheep and rare-breed Welsh pigs can be admired.

Traditional methods of pest control

LLANLLYR

This beautiful Grade II listed Welsh historic garden is located on an ancient site with a long and fascinating history. People have gardened here in the fertile Aeron valley close to the West Wales coast for a thousand years. Celtic saints, Cistercian nuns, Tudor squires, Victorian gentry and farmers have all worked the soil and reaped its reward. The basic structure of the present garden was laid down around 1830, but has undergone considerable restoration and development by present owners Loveday Lewes Gee and her husband Robert since their arrival in 1985.

Wide borders surround the house on the north and east sides. Immediately next to the house is a delightful box garden parterre with a patterned design reminiscent of those popular during the Renaissance. Densely planted shrubberies lead to a colour-themed rose border, which is planted with 500 historic roses on the site of flower borders initially created in the nineteenth century. To the back of the Rose Garden is a walled vegetable garden.

Running parallel to the rose border is a striking Italianate rill and water garden crossed by a little stone bridge. A lake, or large fish pond and a bog garden populated with primulas, gunnera, ferns and irises all add to the aquatic interest.

Sweeping serpentine lawns break up any over-formality and help to separate out individual features, such as an attractive summerhouse and a Celtic inscribed stone. ▸

Rose Garden (*Photo courtesy of Charles Hawes*)

AMOR OMNIA VINCIT

◂ The latter is a scheduled ancient monument and records the gift of a piece of land to the Irish St Madomnuac, an apiarist and disciple of St David at his monastery in Pembrokeshire. Positioned in an alcove at the end of one of the paths and perfectly framed by an Asian rowan *Sorbus commixta*, the stone provides an excellent focal point.

A relatively recent addition to Llanllyr is a labyrinth created using hedges of privet *Ligustrum ovalifolium* and *Escallonia* 'Donard Seedling'. Consisting of a path connecting a series of small garden rooms, its design was inspired by the Dreamer's Journey in William Langland's fourteenth-century poem 'Piers the Plowman'.

In 2002, the owners erected a carved oak column opposite the exit from the labyrinth. The shadow cast by the column at midday marks the months of the year; each month is indicated by a circular sign from the Zodiac. Other features to enjoy include a stage, laburnum arbour and a mound topped by a polished granite sculpture entitled 'Flame' and encircled by drifts of pink-flowering *Persicaria affinis*.

◂ Gazebo with *Cornus controversa* 'Variegata'
(*Photo courtesy of Charles Hawes*)

Llanllyr Rill and Water Garden
(*Photo courtesy of Charles Hawes*)

NATIONAL BOTANIC GARDEN OF WALES

The location for the National Botanic Garden of Wales is the Regency landscaped estate of Middleton Hall, itself set within the beautiful Towy Valley in Carmarthenshire.

Middleton Hall was originally designed and built by the architect Samuel Pepys Cockerell following Sir William Paxton's purchase of the estate in 1789. Around the hall, Paxton created a water-based landscape that included a series of interconnecting lakes, ponds and streams linked by a network of dams, water sluices, bridges and cascades. In 1809, a Neo-Gothic tower was added to the landscape; although erected in honour of Lord Nelson, it actually became known as 'Paxton's Tower'.

In 1931, the hall was completely gutted by fire, leaving only the walls standing. Soon after, the estate fell into disrepair and, in the 1950s, what remained of the hall was demolished. To most people it seemed like the end for the Middleton Estate – it wasn't.

In the closing years of the twentieth century and under the guidance of the Welsh Historic Gardens Trust, an application was made to the Millennium Commission to help fund and build on the Middleton Hall site Britain's first national botanic garden for 200 years.

The garden was opened to the public for the first time on 24 May 2000, and was officially opened on 21 July 2000 by HRH the Prince of Wales. ▸

The National Botanic Garden of Wales in summer

The Great Glass House ▸

NATIONAL BOTANIC GARDEN OF WALES

◀ Covering 568 acres (230 hectares), at its heart is the Great Glasshouse; measuring 360 feet long (110 metres) by 200 feet wide (60 metres), it is the largest single-span glasshouse in the world. Designed by Sir Norman Foster, it rests in the landscape like a giant glistening raindrop. Inside are housed some of the most endangered plants in the world, originating from six Mediterranean climatic regions: Western Australia, Chile, Canary Islands, California, southern Africa and the Mediterranean basin. All the work carried out at the National Botanic Garden of Wales is dedicated to conserving plant diversity.

Located in Middleton's unique and historic double-walled garden is a tropical house full of palms, pineapples, coconuts, cardamom and scores of tropical orchids. Elsewhere there are bog gardens, an apiary, an apothecary garden and numerous ornamental beds and borders.

Today, much of the original Paxton water landscape has been restored and extended by introducing cascades to the western approach to the Great Glasshouse. The original views from the hall to Paxton's Tower have also been restored and the surrounding land is now a National Nature Reserve.

The Japanese Garden

PENPERGWM LODGE

This classic Edwardian house, with its attractive 3-acre (1.2-hectare) RHS recommended garden, is situated on the southern edge of the Black Mountains near Abergavenny in Monmouthshire. Owned by the Boyle family since their arrival at Penpergwm in 1976, the garden has not only been lovingly maintained, but enhanced and developed in a way that pays homage to its Edwardian roots and at the same time moves forward to reflect the changing styles of late twentieth and early twenty-first-century garden design.

The first changes to the structure of the old Edwardian garden were made in the early 1980s with the construction of a stone terrace on the south side of the house, complete with wide steps that lead down to the lawn. This was followed by the creation of another stepped brick terrace on the other side of the house, this time with a central iron-arched dais and seat. At the same time, new brick walls were built to protect the garden from the north and the winds that funnelled down from the mountains. A little later to the north-west of the garden, new shrub and herbaceous borders were created between copper beech hedges and a new fruit orchard planted. ▸

Penpergwm Lodge walled garden with potager

◀ In 1995, the first two terraces became linked when an Italianate parterre of clipped yew and box, designed by Simon Dorrell, was built at the western end of the house. A brick-pillared paved vine and clematis pergola completed the connection. The house was then set off further by the planting in 1997 of a crab apple *Malus sp.* avenue, which was then framed using more beech hedges, which in turn helped to form the westerly view from the house.

In 2002, to mark the Golden Jubilee, an octagonal brick folly tower with weathervane was constructed by James Arbuthnott, whose own garden at Stone House is known as the San Gimignano (city of beautiful towers) of Worcestershire! Penpergwm's tower has extensive views both to the Brecon Beacons National Park and to all corners of the garden.

Since 2002, a semi-circular, oak-pillared and terracotta-roofed summerhouse has been built, the potager in the old kitchen garden redesigned and a Helen Dillon-inspired canal with waterfalls established in the centre of the garden along with a brick-walled and tiled roofed loggia. The final development to date has been the construction of a further brick folly, which frames the view down the canal from the loggia.

◀ Canal with cascade

Penpergwm Lodge brick folly tower

PENRHYN CASTLE

This 48-acre (19-hectare) landscape surrounds one of the most successful examples of Norman Revival architecture. Designed by Thomas Hopper, Penrhyn Castle was built for George Hay Dawkins Pennant between 1822 and 1838 on a hill crest above the university town of Bangor and the Menai Strait, from where its plethora of turrets, towers and battlements dominate the skyline. Given the scale of its surroundings, which include Snowdonia's rugged mountains, the North Wales coastline and Anglesey, the scale of this building had to be big to make a coherent statement of Victorian grandeur, and it does so magnificently. To match the castle's grandeur, Dawkins Pennant developed great sweeps of parkland around its Virginia creeper-clad ramparts, which he planted with pines, oaks (evergreen and Welsh), beech and lime. Queen Victoria added to the collection when she planted a giant redwood *Sequoiadendron giganteum* on a visit to Penrhyn Castle in October 1859. The tree still stands and is just a short walk from the main National Trust visitor entrance.

Away from the castle, the parkland gradually gives way to groves of dense vegetation, where meandering paths spill out into a succession of glades containing the ruins of a 'Gothic chapel', banks of heather, a 30-foot-tall (9-metre) forest of mimosa *Acacia dealbata* and giant rhododendrons by the score including *R. arboreum*, *R. macabeanum*, *R. barbatum* and *R. decorum*.

Eventually the ground drops away to the west and, as it does, the temperature rises and Penrhyn's walled garden appears. ▸

Penrhyn Castle Fuschia Walk

Penrhyn Castle with Queen Victoria's giant redwood in the foreground ▸

❋ PENRHYN CASTLE

◀ Sheltered and intimate, there are no grandiose statements here, just a wonderful collection of tender woody plants and climbers, the latter scrambling over the inner walls and balustrade between formal terrace and four rectangular sloping lawns. In the 1930s, Lady Penrhyn reworked the original Victorian parterre of the upper terrace, introducing box-edged beds, lily ponds, fountains and loggia. On the lawns below are massed an eclectic collection of shrubs and trees, including *Eucryphia cordifolia*, *Drimys winteri*, flowering dogwoods *Cornus kousa*, Persian ironwoods *Parrotia persica* and *Sciadopitys verticillata*. The sloping ground is halted for a moment by an ironwork pergola dripping with *Fuchsia magellanica* 'Riccartonii' and *Clematis* 'Jackmanii Superba' before abruptly dropping away into a bog garden complete with tree ferns, gunnera, bamboos and swamp cypress *Taxodium distichum*. This is a place to linger and soak up the *Secret Garden* atmosphere, far away from the hustle and bustle of the castle ... perhaps Lord and Lady Penrhyn did just that!

Penrhyn Castle walled garden

PICTON CASTLE

Originally built at the end of the thirteenth century by Sir John Wogan and still inhabited by his descendants, Picton Castle is situated close to the beautiful Cleddau Estuary, known locally as the 'hidden waterway' and just a few miles from the Pembrokeshire coastline of West Wales.

The building is unusual in design, being half fortified manor house and half medieval castle. From the outside, its four symmetrically spaced half round towers and gatehouse flanked by two further towers look like a miniature version of one of the great Welsh castles, such as Conwy or Caernarfon. However, on entering, it becomes apparent that Picton does not have an inner courtyard or keep, but rather a series of rooms typical of a grand country house.

The climate at Picton is benign and ideal for growing a wide range of exotic plants. Surrounding the property is over 40 acres (16 hectares) of grounds, which include one of the largest collections of cultivated plants in West Wales. Owned and managed by a registered charity called the Picton Garden Trust, many of the plants are to be found within beautiful woodland gardens that radiate out from the castle. ▸

Picton Castle and grounds from the air

PICTON CASTLE

◀ Picton is renowned for its collection of springtime flowering shrubs, including a large and important rhododendron collection, many of which bloom above a sea of bluebells in Picton's oak and beech woodland. One of its finest specimens is the biggest rhododendron 'Old Port' in cultivation, which was raised as a hybrid of *Rhododendron catawbiense* before 1865. With rich plum-purple flowers speckled with crimson-black markings, it is regarded as one of the most beautiful rhododendrons in existence. Former Picton head gardener Leo Ekkes bred several new rhododendron cultivars including 'Jubilee' and 'Picton Maid'.

Alongside the rhododendrons, Chilean lantern bushes *Crinodendron hookerianum*, avenues of myrtle and South American Eucryphias carry the flowering displays on into summer, which is when Picton's walled garden with its herbs and summer-flowering borders come into their own. Here, on hot summer days, a pond and fountain create a cool, calming oasis.

In recent years, head gardener Roddie Milne has created an atmospheric tree fern glade and planted many species of bamboo to give all-year-round structure and interest to the garden. A maze, woodland walks past 300-year-old oaks and exotic conifers such as a gigantic *Cryptomeria japonica* 'Elegans', two giant redwoods *Sequoiadendron giganteum* and a fine specimen of the 'Dawn redwood fossil tree' *Metasequoia glyptostroboides* all add to the beauty and interest of this garden.

◀ Rhododendrons and azaleas

Spring at Picton Castle

PLANTASIA

It would be easy to be snobbish about the inclusion of Plantasia in a book that defines itself as being a serious portrayal of the very best gardens that Wales has to offer. After all, it is a modern-day, council-run 'plant theme park', which is set amid a shopping centre in the middle of Swansea, and yes, it does do weddings and children's birthday parties too. It is, dare I say, not the obvious choice for a U3A garden club outing or RHS affiliated horticultural society afternoon visit. However, perhaps it should be because Wales' collective horticultural 'offering' is much the richer for having Plantasia in the same way that Cornwall is the richer for having the Eden Project.

Plantasia is not some poorly designed greenhouse with a substandard collection of ill-maintained hot-house flowers. This is a serious botanical establishment that not only houses one of the finest collections of rainforest and arid-zone (desert) plants in Britain (outside the major botanic gardens), but is also doing a tremendous job in helping all of us, including many schoolchildren, to understand and appreciate just how crucial plants and rainforest ecosystems are to the world and our place within it. ▸

Pool with carp
(Image courtesy of Alan Gregg)

Plantasia Rainforest Walk ▸
(Image courtesy of Alan Gregg)

◀ Within its humid interior, Plantasia grows close on 1,500 different plant species and cultivars ranging from giant tropical bamboos to grapefruit, and most of them have benefits to mankind over and above the generic plant benefits of oxygen production, carbon absorption and climate control.

Here, within the space of an hour or so, you can see an astonishing and beautiful collection of exotic plants and learn some fascinating plant-based facts: not only are present-day cycads descendants of plants that lived on earth over 200 million years ago, they are also the mainstay of sago puddings too! Juice from the petals of hibiscus flowers were formerly used to blacken the hair and eyebrows, and also served as shoe blacking. Coarse fibres from the fleshy succulent leaves of the agave plant *Agave americana* were used 8,000 years ago for making fishing nets. Contrary to popular belief, bananas are not trees but one of the largest herbaceous plants on earth.

Once you have absorbed enough information, you can visit an authentic recreation of an Amazonian rainforest dwelling, where you really get a sense of how different our homes are to some regions of the world. There are also examples of rainforest-based mammals, insects and birds and an aquarium to enjoy.

The tropical rainforest zone at Plantasia (*Image courtesy of Alan Gregg*)

❁ PLAS BRONDANW

In 1904, architect Sir Clough Williams-Ellis was given Plas Brondanw by his father and immediately set about creating a landscaped garden around his sixteenth-century ancestral home. 'It became a passion and obsession if you like,' wrote Sir Clough, 'it was for Brondanw's sake that I worked and stinted, for its sake I chiefly hoped to prosper. A cheque of ten pounds would come in and I would order yew hedging to that extent, a cheque for twenty and I would pave a further piece of terrace'.

His work at Plas Brondanw gave Sir Clough the confidence to embark in 1925 on his larger project at nearby Portmeirion. Larger it may be and undeniably more famous, however the garden at Plas Brondanw should be considered of equal importance to his Italianate creation, for it is brilliantly conceived and designed. Inspired by the Arts & Crafts movement, Plas Brondanw is reminiscent of Hidcote with its intimate rooms enclosed by dense, close-clipped yew hedging. However, this is not a garden that forces you to look inwards – far from it. Sir Clough understood that the majestic Snowdonian landscape must be embraced, so throughout the garden you are constantly reminded of what lies beyond. Hazy-blue ridgelines are glimpsed through archways and dramatic reveals appear at the end of pathways, such as the one perfectly aligned on the Matterhorn-like peak of Cnicht. ▸

Bronze warrior on column surrounded by hydrangeas

◂ Of course the foreground had to be engaging and interesting, otherwise the garden becomes little more than a viewing platform for the wider landscape. Sir Clough used all his architectural skill to ensure the right balance. Urns, statues, fountains, orangery, gateways and steps are all here, beautifully designed and placed. Where metalwork is found, it is painted in the estate colours of pale turquoise-blue and yellow, a reference to the fact that a sandy shoreline and sea once lapped just below the garden's boundary.

It was architect and garden designer Harold Peto who said, 'a garden isn't a garden if it doesn't include architecture as well as plants'; perhaps so, but Sir Clough resisted the temptation to crowd the space with ornamentation in a way that stifled botanical interest. Bright red *Tropaeolum speciosum* cheerily appears among dark green foliage, Japanese anemones and Welsh poppies soften walls, fuchsias drip from balustrades, large-leaved hostas and primulas fringe pathways and flamboyant yew topiary punctuates straight-lined hedging.

Make no mistake, this is a masterpiece of a garden and one that should be on every garden-lover's itinerary.

◂ View to Moel Ddu

Yew topiary hedge

PLAS CADNANT

Plas Cadnant is located at the head of the beautiful hidden valley of Cwm Cadnant on the Isle of Anglesey. Tumbling and frothing its way through the valley is the Afon Cadnant, which feeds crystal-clear freshwater into the tidal salinity of the Menai Strait less than 1 mile away. From the point where the two waters meet, rising above a series of delightful mid-strait rocky outcrops and islets, is the stunning outline of Thomas Telford's suspension bridge, built in 1826 to link the rugged mountain-lands of Snowdonia with the fertile plains of Ynys Môn.

Originally a farm dating from the sixteenth century, by the Victorian era Plas Cadnant was a gentleman's country estate. At its heart stood a 2-acre (0.8 hectare) south-east-facing walled garden with rectangular pool. Beyond the wall a network of paths led through the valley woodland, which was planted in the picturesque style with a mixture of ornamental trees, shrubs and other plants.

Sadly, by the latter part of the twentieth century, both maintenance and manpower were in short supply and when the property came up for sale in the 1990s, it was in relatively poor condition.

It was then that Staffordshire farmer Anthony Tavernor came to Anglesey and purchased the estate. Part of his interest lay with the neglected cottages and garden, which he felt could be returned to their former glory. ▸

◂ The orangery with hydrangeas

Double herbaceous borders

◂ He began the huge task of restoration without any formal horticultural training, but with enormous determination.

Having achieved his first task of restoring the cottages and former farmhouse, he turned his attention to the walled garden, rebuilding tumbled-down walls, felling self-seeded sycamores and sowing lawns in the process. The rectangular pool was resealed, filled and surrounded with Bergenia 'Overture', and, at strategic places throughout the walled garden, yew trees were planted to become future topiary.

Today, the walled garden restoration is complete and the original network of garden paths that meandered through the valley have been reinstated and the valley planted with thousands of fabulous specimens, many of them rare or unusual. However, the atmosphere is still that of a private garden. Care has been taken to plant for a long season of interest; there are early spring flowering shrubs such as daphnes, camellias, rhododendrons and pieris, beautiful herbaceous borders in summer and many unusual hydrangeas, maples and other deciduous trees for autumn colour.

In recent years a splendid oak-framed visitor centre and traditional tea room have also been built.

◂ Pineapple pit house

The restored walled garden at Plas Cadnant

PLAS NEWYDD

This superb 40-acre (16-hectare) garden, the bones of which were laid out in the late eighteenth century following recommendations made by Humphry Repton in his Red Book dated 1798/99, surrounds the ancestral home of the Marquess of Anglesey. Set amid beautiful scenery just above the tidal reaches of the Menai Strait on the eastern edge of the Isle of Anglesey, Plas Newydd is blessed with stunning views along the North Wales coast and across the Strait to the wooded shoreline of the Vaynol estate with the majestic Snowdonian mountains rising beyond.

From the garden, trails follow the Anglesey shoreline in the direction of Robert Stephenson's Britannia railway bridge while a network of internal garden footpaths meander back and forth across 'West Indies', an area comprised of flowing lawns and island beds full of choice flowering shrubs such as *Enkianthus campanulatus*, *Osmanthus delavayi* and *Kalmia latifolia*.

As with so many Welsh coastal gardens, summers here are sunny and cool and winters mild and wet, which means the pallet of plants that thrive here is wider than in most UK gardens. This is nowhere more evident than in 'Australasia', a secluded part of the garden frequented by the native red squirrel population and positioned to the west of the house. ▸

Spring in the Dell

Magnolia sprengeri 'Diva' ▸

◂ Planted in 1981, 'Australia' contains a fine selection of southern hemisphere plants, including eucalyptus, nothofagus, olearia, pittosporum, grevillea and griselinia. Given these plants are not forty years old, it is astonishing how large they have grown, especially the eucalyptus, although sadly, several were destroyed during the gales of February 2014.

In spring throughout the garden, banks of camellias, deciduous azaleas and rhododendrons bloom in the shelter of giant Himalayan magnolias including a 60-feet tall (18-metre) *Magnolia sprengeri* 'Diva', the Goddess Magnolia. Such is the weight of blooms along the lower branches, they rest among the topmost flowers of the shrubs that grow beneath. A mile away from the main garden and accessible via a path along the Menai Strait is the late 6th Marquess of Anglesey's rhododendron wood. Begun in the 1930s it contains an overgrown, wild but exciting collection of rare and unusual rhododendrons and other spring-flowering shrubs.

In summer, massed displays of 800 hydrangeas replace the rhododendrons; however, the main focus of attention shifts to the recently renovated formal terraces to the east of the house. Here, fountains, pools and close-clipped evergreens cultivate an Italianate atmosphere while the lower terraces positively zing with hot-coloured herbaceous borders.

View from the garden across the Menai Strait to the mountains of Snowdonia

PLAS NEWYDD LLANGOLLEN

Famous as the home of Lady Eleanor Butler and Miss Sarah Ponsonby (otherwise known as the 'Ladies of Llangollen'), Plas Newydd is a living textbook of fashionable garden design spanning three centuries. The ladies first arrived at Pen-y-Maes cottage in 1780 and remained until Eleanor's death in 1829. During this time, they transformed and enlarged the cottage, renaming it Plas Newydd (New Hall) in the process.

They described their life here as one of 'sweet and delicious retirement'; however, they were certainly not idle and their work on the house and garden captured the imagination of Regency society. Over the years many travellers, including the Duke of Wellington, Sir Walter Scott and Wordsworth, broke their journey at Llangollen and strolled the gardens before taking tea with the ladies.

Long after their deaths, their legacy was still attracting attention. In 1854, George Borrow visited during his tour of the Principality, later described in his seminal work, *Wild Wales*. Having spent the day walking the Berwyn mountains and exploring the medieval ruins of Castell Dinas Bran (both of which provide a superb backdrop to Plas Newydd), he arrived at the property, where he met an old man who remembered the ladies and the small Welsh cottage, which they turned into a Gothic fantasy of white walls, elaborately carved oak and stained glass. ▸

Plas Newydd Llangollen with Castell Dinas Bran in the background

◀ The garden the ladies originally created lies in a wooded dell alongside the house and was designed in the 'picturesque style' of the day. They introduced meandering paths, romantic vistas, leafy bowers, rustic seats, arching bridges across Cyflymen stream, a summerhouse where they kept favourite books and a gothic recess into which they set a stone font gleaned from nearby Valle Crucis Abbey. Much of this garden had long since disappeared, but, since 2002, a restoration programme has reinstated some of its original appearance – likewise the Ladies' Georgian shrubbery, which lies immediately to the rear of the house and was planted with lilac, laburnum and white-flowering broom.

The formal gardens, parterre and flamboyant topiary directly in front of the house are of much later design. During the ladies' tenure, this was a meadow grazed by cosws, but in 1910 owner G. H. Robertson, influenced by Edwardian Arts & Crafts garden design, planted right up to the house in an attempt to blend artistry, architecture and horticulture into one seamless landscape. The stone circle nearby was built for the Gorsedd of Bard's ceremonies at the Llangollen Eisteddfod in 1908.

◀ Flamboyant yew topiary

Gothic recess with stone font

PLAS TAN Y BWLCH

Located high above the swift-flowing waters of the Afon Dwyryd, with spectacular views across the Vale of Ffestiniog to the village of Maentwrog, Plas Tan y Bwlch ('mansion under the pass' in English) was home to one-time slate quarry owners the Oakeley family from 1789 until 1961. Currently owned and used as a study centre by the Snowdonia National Park Authority, the mansion is surrounded by 13 acres (5.2 hectares) of formal and woodland gardens, much of which was laid out for William Edward Oakeley by his head gardener, John Roberts, in a period lasting from the 1880s until the beginning of the twentieth century. The wider scenery beyond the garden is not Victorian in design and clearly shows influences of the eighteenth and early nineteenth-century picturesque landscape movement.

Some of the best views of the garden are obtained from the broad terraces positioned directly to the south of the main house. From here, billowing heads of enormous Himalayan tree rhododendrons, in particular *Rhododendron arboreum*, produce cerise-pink clouds of bloom in April and May. Given their stature, these particular specimens are likely to predate William Edward Oakeley's garden and may well be close to 200 years old.

Below the terraces, sunny, sheltered borders support a good range of tender exotic plants. ▸

Plas Tan y Bwlch Mansion

Plas Tan y Bwlch in springtime ▸

◀ These include Mrytle *Luma apiculata* from Chile, with its attractive cinnamon-coloured bark, the false camellia tree *Stewartia pseudocamellia* from Japan, *Clerodendrum bungei* from China, which produces bright red fragrant flowers in August and September, and *Magnolia grandiflora*, the evergreen Bullbay magnolia from the southern states of the USA. A small, stone-built gothic-style building below the eastern corner of the terrace was a gardeners' bothy and was probably built in the 1880s when the terrace was extended.

Further away from the borders and terraces, the garden becomes less formal, with long banks of deciduous azaleas intermingling with Japanese maples. Paths wander across grassy slopes and pass small pools, giant Indian cedars *Cedrus deodara* and a fine pocket-handkerchief tree *Davidia involucrata* before disappearing into the ornamental woodland beyond.

The western end of the woodland garden was badly affected by 100mph winds and storms in February 2014. More than forty mature oaks and conifers were blown down, crushing shrubs and damaging pathways. Since then, a programme of clearance and restoration has begun.

Located on the terraces are a conservatory tea room and a small museum, where visitors can watch a video presentation on the history of this unique estate and the people who created it.

Rhododendron arboreum

South-facing borders and bothy ▶

PLAS YN RHIW

The road to Plas yn Rhiw rides the undulating hills and valleys of the Lleyn Peninsula before revealing spectacular vistas along the sweeping 6-mile (11-km) shoreline of Porth Neigwl (Hell's Mouth). Located towards the westerly end of the bay and seemingly exposed to winds and storms roaring in from the Irish Sea, this unique 1-acre (0.4-hectare) garden is in fact sheltered by surrounding woodland and the slopes of nearby Mynydd Rhiw.

It is a place of rare unspoilt beauty, something recognised by the three Keating sisters, Honora, Lorna and Eileen, and their widowed mother, Constance. In 1938, Constance purchased the property, which included a dilapidated seventeenth-century granite house, along with 58 acres (23 hectares) of surrounding land. Having restored the house, the family embarked upon the garden. A map of 1844 showed there had once been a garden laid out in formal Victorian style; however, by 1938, this was completely overgrown. The original box hedging and some of the larger shrubs remained so the sisters reclaimed these and began to plant, using a combination of cottage-garden flowers, bulbs, shrubs and trees. In time the garden became an Aladdin's cave of exotic plants, local wildflowers and ferns, which the women admired and encouraged. ▸

Plas yn Rhiw house

Box-bordered pathways ▸

◀ Few records survive of their endeavours. However, in a 1963 plant catalogue, Honora wrote, '*Magnolia mollicomata*, planted by me in 1946, is for the first time covered in perfect blooms, over 150 counted on 7th April'.

The property was given to the National Trust in the 1940s, although the women continued to live and garden there. As the decades passed, maintenance became a struggle and by 1981, when Lorna, the last Miss Keating, died, the garden was in a graceful state of decline and the trust began a programme of sympathetic restoration.

It is to their credit that today the atmosphere is still one of a private and much-loved family home and garden. Wherever you are, the spirit of these inspirational ladies is tangible and it is easy to visualise them sewing in the parlour or weeding the terraces.

On entering the garden, which the trust manages organically, intimate pathways squeezed by box hedging lead you down a series of terraces where spring-flowering camellias and rhododendrons give way to sweet, summer-scented mock-orange, roses and clethra, while sublime blue-shaded hydrangeas and bushes dripping with fuchsia blooms carry the colour and interest well into autumn. This is a truly magical garden and one set to some of the finest seascapes in Wales.

View to Hell's Mouth

PORTMEIRION

Portmeirion, the fabulous fantasy Italianate-style village designed by architect Sir Clough Williams-Ellis, is well known as the setting for the cult 1960s TV series, *The Prisoner*. It is also the place of origin for Portmeirion pottery and has more recently become the venue for an up and coming music and arts festival known simply as 'Number 6'. However, what isn't widely known is that Portmeirion has one of the most unique and diverse collections of gardens and plants in the Principality.

The main reason for this diversity is the microclimate that exists here. Portmeirion's headland location, proximity to the sea and the warm, moist air resulting from the North Atlantic Drift keeps the garden (relatively) mild in winter. This means that tender and, in some cases, sub-tropical plants will grow here more readily than in many other parts of the British Isles. Proof of this can be seen by the number of Chinese Chusan Palms *Trachycarpus fortuneii*, Mediterranean *Phillyrea latifolia*, Australasian bottlebrushes *Callistemon sp*, South African agapanthus and South American myrtles *Luma apiculata*, which grow in the piazzas, avenues, beds and borders surrounding Sir Clough's eclectic mix of Gothic, Renaissance and Victorian buildings.

However, just beyond the village is a very different landscape altogether. ▸

Portmeirion Village Garden

◀ A 70-acre (28-hectare) woodland called Y Gwyllt ('the wild place' in English) conceals from view a secret valley containing lakes, oriental follies and bridges, headland viewpoints, gigantic Japanese cedars with golden-brown peeling bark and dense mature vegetation reminiscent of the Bhutanese foothills of the Himalayas.

Y Gwyllt was initially planted by Victorian tenants H. S. Westmacott and Sir William Fothergill Cooke, as an arboretum and woodland garden. From 1900 to 1941, George Henry Caton Haigh, a recognised world authority on flowering plants (especially rhododendrons) from the Himalayan region, augmented their earlier collection. Many of Haigh's original plants still survive, including rhododendron species such as *Rhododendron falconeri* and *Rhododendron arboreum* with some specimens now over 40 feet (12 metres) tall, as well as Portmeirion-bred cultivars such as the beautiful red-flowering *Rhododendron* 'Gwyllt King'.

Here also are many tender southern hemisphere plants, including a magnificent specimen of the New Zealand evergreen *Griselinia littoralis*, nicknamed by Sir Clough as 'The Dancing Tree' because of its outstretched limbs, which seem to dance in the wind.

For those who want a longer walk, a number of pathways run right through Y Gwyllt and out to the coast, where magnificent views open out across Tremadog Bay to William Madocks' causeway and Porthmadog beyond.

◀ Japanese-style features in Y Gwyllt

Springtime in Y Gwyllt

❈ POWIS CASTLE

Powis Castle is probably one of the best-known and admired gardens in Wales, and rightly so. It is without doubt one of the brightest jewels in the Principality's horticultural crown – and for that matter the crown of its current owners, the National Trust. The drama, atmosphere and architectural splendour of Powis is evident from the moment you pass its ornamental wrought-iron gates and allow your eyes to move upwards across an ever-rising canopy of exotic trees, sumptuous Italianate terracing and mounded domes of sombre yews until finally you reach the pink-stoned castellated fortress on the skyline. Once the home of Welsh Princes and Earls, this formidable twelfth-century border castle now stands proud above 25 acres (10 hectares) of glorious gardens full of bold and diverse plantings.

Originally laid out in the 1680s and based upon formal designs by William Winde, this cliffhanger of a garden has since evolved under successive generations of the Herbert family, the Earls of Powis. There are influences aplenty here, including Renaissance Italy, seen so vividly in the flamboyant balustrades, alcoves, statuary and urns. In fact, the terraces are believed to have been inspired by those of the Palace of St Germain-en-Laye near Paris, where the 1st Marquis of Powis sat in exile with King James II after the Glorious Revolution of 1688, which put William of Orange on the British throne. ▸

First view of the terraces

Formal terraces climb the hillside ▸

◀ Notable terrace features include dramatic yew topiary, an orangery and grotto-like niches full of tender and deliciously scented rhododendrons such as 'Lady Alice Fitzwilliam'.

Beyond the terraces, changes were made to the original landscape in the late eighteenth century and these are attributed to William Emes, who laid out the parkland in typical picturesque English landscape style, but somehow those of Lancelot 'Capability' Brown's persuasion never quite managed to get their hands on these remarkable terraces.

In the nineteenth and early twentieth centuries, Lady Violet Herbert, wife of the 4th Earl of Powis, used the structure of the garden and the planting opportunities it offered to overlay with ornamental plants and flowers, many of which were recent introductions from the far reaches of the British Empire. Unusual and tender plants thrived in the shelter of the walls, alcoves and hedges, and in 1911 the formal kitchen garden was transformed into a beautiful flower garden. Today, fuchsias, cestrums, abutilons, cistus and *Carpenteria californica* adorn the terraces, while wisteria, clematis and numerous climbing roses, including *Rosa banksiae* 'Lutea', ramble at will.

Parkland beyond the garden

Yew topiary ▶

RIDLER'S GARDEN

Whatever is written about this uncompromising formal half-acre (0.2-hectare) garden, set within an urban location behind a terraced house on the outskirts of Swansea, it will not do justice to the care, attention to detail and design skills of its creator, graphic designer Tony Ridler. Mind you, Ridler's Garden is not to everyone's liking; if you enjoy informality, the serendipity of a self-sown plant and relaxed lines, then perhaps this is not for you, but even then, it is difficult not to have a sneaking admiration for the way that nature has been controlled here. Substitute circus ringmaster's whip for sharply-honed secateurs and you may begin to get the picture.

The garden has been subdivided by densely planted and closely clipped evergreen hedges and black walls to create small compartments, each with its own unique twist or focal point. Tony initially found inspiration from Lawrence Johnston's garden at Hidcote in Gloucestershire, where design is key and an 'Alice in Wonderland' sense of surprise builds as one garden room leads into another. Here, vistas open where least expected and sudden reveals appear around every corner.

Ridler's Garden is introspective in that there is no 'borrowed landscape'. Your eye is constantly immersed within a world of strongly sculpted architectural evergreen shapes; blocks, spirals, orbs and sight

Sense of tranquillity reminiscent of Japanese gardens

lines abound. It is truly a design masterclass in the use of form, structure and balance. However, despite this formality, there is also a sense of tranquillity here, in a way that is reminiscent of the dry raked gravel and clipped topiary gardens of Kyoto.

Some of the 'eye grabbers' you will have seen before (lollipop-form Portuguese laurel, box balls and pyramids); others are superbly original, such as exquisitely crafted topiary spirals mulched with white cockleshells and stone-sett geometric-patterned curves rising from the ground to be seamlessly replicated and continued within the sweeping lines of clipped evergreens.

You could be forgiven for thinking that there are no flowers here at all, but there are, including carefully placed containers of red tulips and purple and white fritillaries in spring, and pink penstemon and orange marigolds in summer, all offset by dark grey slate or light grey gravel. Colour is also introduced into the garden through foliage; the use of purple-leaved phormiums, ophiopogon grasses and alternating purple and green salad leaves is truly sublime. Standard figs add height to the garden and there is even a pocket handkerchief tree *Davidia involucrata* rising from a sea of large beach pebbles.

Ridler's Garden: where design is key

SINGLETON BOTANICAL GARDENS

With both Clyne Gardens and Plantasia close by, and several other well-maintained parks within the city, Swansea is without doubt the municipal horticultural capital of Wales. Much of the credit for this must go to Swansea City Council, who have not only continued to maintain but indeed develop and enhance the botanical establishments within their charge. Perhaps the jewel in Swansea's horticultural crown is Singleton Botanical Gardens. An excellent 5-acre (2-hectare) site with an extensive plant collection containing ornamental gardens, herbaceous borders, rockeries, herbs and Mediterranean plants, rose beds, an interesting collection of trees and shrubs, a Japanese bridge and waterfall, lily ponds, a bog garden and recently erected temperate and tropical glasshouses containing an extensive range of orchids, bromeliads and epiphytes.

The history of the site goes back to 1847 when John Henry Vivian purchased Veranda House for his son Henry Hussey Vivian. By 1851, the walled garden had become the productive kitchen and flower garden for the Vivian family, and by 1853 the Singleton estate, as it had now become, had amalgamated some twelve farms and amassed around 250 acres (101 hectares) of land. Henry Hussey Vivian, who later became the 1st Lord Swansea, lived in part of the estate now called the Ornamental Gardens, and along with his wife, Sarah, who was an enthusiastic gardener, established many of the older plant collections that exist at Singleton today. ▸

Bedding at its best
(Image courtesy of Alan Gregg)

Springtime bulb displays ▸
(Image courtesy of Alan Gregg)

◀ The County Borough Council purchased Singleton in 1919 for use as a public park. Daniel Bliss, who had trained at the Royal Botanical Gardens Kew, was the driving force behind this purchase, and from early 1920 began to oversee the transformation of the park and garden. The present layout has much to do with his vision and plans. The main herbaceous border was originally laid out and planted by Bliss in 1921, and this is what greets you warmly as you enter the garden in summer today. In the central rectangle, the display beds have collections of iris, dahlias, chrysanthemums, sweet peas, carnations, asters, delphiniums and penstemons. Other beds display high quality bedding schemes. Although the gardens are perhaps at their most stunning during summer, there is something to see throughout the year. Collections of magnolias, camellias and an internationally famous collection of rhododendrons ensure flowering and colour in spring; even in winter the garden has a lot to offer, with up to 200 different plants having been recorded in flower during the Christmas season.

Herbaceous borders with cannas and bananas (*Image courtesy of Alan Gregg*)

ST FAGANS CASTLE GARDENS

St Fagans is perhaps best known for its excellent open-air Welsh National History Museum, where more than forty historical buildings depict how the people of Wales have lived, worked, gardened, played and worshipped from the Iron Age through to the nineteenth century. To the eastern end of the 104-acre (42-hectare) site is St Fagans Castle, a Grade I listed Elizabethan manor house surrounded by a series of fascinating gardens reflecting several periods of garden history.

Approached through woodland of magnificent gun-barrel-straight beech trees, the first glimpse of the gardens reveals the castle high on the crest of an escarpment and broad Italianate terraces descending towards a rectangular pool. The pool is in fact four fish ponds, each separated by a turf covered dam and dating back to at least 1766. Originally created as a 'fish farm' and stocked with carp, bream and tench, they would have provided a regular source of food for those living in the castle. To reach the pools the path meanders through an arboretum of exotic trees and shrubs, including fragrant-flowering deciduous azaleas, which are an absolute joy in springtime. ▸

St Fagans Italian Garden

◂ Fringing the pools are ornamental moisture-loving plants, including *Gunnera manicata* and yellow flag iris *Iris pseudacorus*. Further upstream a water garden, designed by the well-known Victorian rockwork family Pulham & Co., divides the water past a mid-stream rocky island inhabited by two elfin statues.

There are five main terraces between the pools and the castle, all designed around a framework of stone balustrades, yew topiary, white Grecian urns, lead statuary, wooden trellising and gravel pathways. They are all softened by the clever use of flowering shrubs and climbers, including the beautiful Chilean coral plant *Berberidopsis corallina*.

Beyond the terraces, avenues of pleached limes, planted in 1901, lead to a large square walled garden that is broken down into a series of compartments, which include a parterre, bowling green, flower garden, herb garden, mulberry grove and rose garden, appropriately called The Rosery. Restored to its formal Edwardian layout in the latter years of the twentieth century, it is faithfully planted with rose varieties known to have been growing here during that period. The more recently restored Italian Garden, opened by HRH the Prince of Wales in 2003, provides an exquisite tranquil space containing a raised pool, lawns and citrus fruits growing in Versailles-style white-painted boxes designed to allow any one of the four sides to be removed in order to prune the roots.

◂ St Fagans Italianate terraces

St Fagans Mulberry Grove

THE GARDEN HOUSE

There are some gardens that deserve to be much better known than they are, and The Garden House near Erbistock, Wrexham, is one of them. The modesty shown by owner Simon Wingett and his family belies just how good this garden is. Little more than a cow field in the early 1990s when Simon first received planning permission to build the house, the garden's creation owes much to Simon's mother, who designed and then established this horticultural gem with an eye to four-season appeal and an emphasis on colour.

There was no grand plan; as ideas evolved, so grass was removed, borders dug, hedges planted and garden rooms established. From the start it was important to establish colour in the garden, to fill the gap caused by the fading summer herbaceous borders; the plant considered most suitable for this role was hydrangea. Shrubby and accommodating, hydrangeas grow well on the site, and before too long they became the main focus for the whole garden.

Today, The Garden House hosts one of the finest hydrangea collections in the country and has been given National Collection (Plant Heritage) status. However, do not think that the only time to visit is from midsummer into early autumn when these flamboyant plants are at their best – far from it. The imaginative designs and clever use of colour, form and texture throughout make this garden worth visiting at any time of year.

Some of the most successful innovations involve the sculpting of evergreens and conifers. Within the 'colour circle garden', surrounding box, yew and golden privet have been clipped to provide an impression of looking out from within a coronet or crown. ▸

◂ *Berberidopsis corallina*

Hydrangea collection

◂ At its very centre, a bed of densely planted bergenias cluster around a giant spherical orb reminiscent of an allium seed head.

There are a further nine garden rooms or areas, all displaying stimulating and clever use of seemingly everyday plants, including a collection of glaucous-blue conifers, which bounce their colouring off beds top-dressed with Bethesda-purple slate – simple, but so effective.

This is not a garden that is allowed to 'rest on its laurels'. Mother's horticultural energy has been passed on to Simon Wingett, who is currently developing both a garden room devoted to *Hydrangea paniculata* 'Limelight' and a hydrangea wheel, with pathway 'spokes' leading to a central viewing position. Plants can also be purchased from The Garden House's own nursery, which, quite naturally, specialises in hydrangeas.

◂ The water garden

The Coronet Garden

TREBORTH BOTANIC GARDEN

Treborth Botanic Garden is located within an Area of Outstanding Natural Beauty (AONB) alongside the Menai Strait just 2 miles west of the North Wales university town of Bangor. The site was originally designed in the 1840s by Sir Joseph Paxton as a pleasure garden for the Chester and Holyhead Railway Company, and included a cascade and an avenue of lime trees. It was intended to become part of a much larger garden called 'Britannia Park', an entrepreneurial Victorian development that would include a grand hotel, glasshouses and conservatories (in the style of those Paxton designed for the Crystal Palace near London), and a brand new railway station on the main line to Holyhead. However, due to financial problems, the scheme never came to fruition and the site eventually reverted to grassland and woodland.

In the 1960s, the 45-acre (18-hectare) site was purchased by the University of Bangor, who began developing it as a collection of plants for study by the Department of Botany. Since then, the garden has become an important resource for students of Bangor's School of Biological Sciences, the School of Environment, Natural Resources and Geography as well as many primary and secondary schools. ▸

Acer griseum in the island beds

Mediterranean plants such as branched asphodel ▸

◂ The garden is also open to the public throughout the year and receives on average more than 35,000 visitors per annum.

Today, the garden contains more than 2,000 native and exotic ornamental plant species contained within a series of island beds and borders set within well-manicured lawns and augmented by pools and a rock garden. Due to Treborth's close proximity to the coast, winters are relatively mild here and tender plants from warmer regions of the world thrive in the moist warm air. These include the evergreen Chilean Mayten tree *Maytenus boaria*, Branched Asphodel *Asphodelus ramosus* from the Mediterranean and North Africa (a perennial herb which produces beautiful white fragrant flower spikes in spring and early summer) and the yucca-like *Beschorneria yuccoides* from Mexico. There are also several glasshouses providing protection for less hardy species and an underground Rhizotron, the largest in Europe, where plant root systems can be studied. Ancient woodland containing red squirrels on a Site of Special Scientific Interest (SSSI) fringes the rocky shoreline of the garden and offers access to the All Wales Coastal Footpath, from where glimpses of Thomas Telford's suspension bridge and Robert Stephenson's Britannia Bridge (built in 1850 to carry the railway from London to Holyhead) can be admired.

The rock garden at Treborth Botanic Garden

TREDEGAR HOUSE

Tredegar House was originally built in the 1670s for the highly influential and political Morgan family, as a statement of their wealth and power. It became one of the grandest houses of the Restoration period in the whole of Wales. The property remained with the family until 1951, when it was sold to the Catholic Church and became a convent school. In 1974, it was purchased by Newport Council, which caused Tredegar to become known as 'the grandest council house in Britain'! In March 2012, management of both the house and 90 acres (36 hectares) of gardens and parkland was taken over by the National Trust and a programme of updating and development began.

The original approach to the house crossed a 1,000-acre (404-hectare) deer park planted with avenues of oak, walnut and chestnut; the deer have gone and the park is much smaller but several of the trees remain – venerable hollow giants providing valuable habitats for bats, owls and insects. In 1788, landscape architect Adam Mickle added further features to the park, including a lake. Almost a century later, the lake was fringed with Victorian plantings of giant redwoods *Sequoiadendron giganteum*, Corsican pines *Pinus nigra*, and deodar cedars *Cedrus deodara*, all of which provide dappled shade for a delightful lakeside walk between billowing clouds of rhododendrons. ▸

Orangery Garden

◂ Close to the house are formal walled gardens divided into three enclosures, the first of which is the Orchard Garden. Here, surrounded by red-brick pockmarked walls, are vegetable beds, fruit trees and a series of attractive ornamental borders containing interesting shrubs and perennials, including *Solanum crispum* 'Glasnevin', Chinese bananas *Musa basjoo* and a whole array of rambling roses, which fill the enclosure with their heady sweet fragrance.

Beyond the wall lies the Cedar Garden, which is dominated by a magnificent cedar of Lebanon *Cedrus libani* and an obelisk, surrounded by yew hedging, built to honour Sir Briggs, the horse that Godfrey Morgan rode into battle at the Charge of the Light Brigade. The final enclosure is the Orangery Garden; here, facing south-west, is the restored orangery originally built in the late seventeenth century by Thomas Morgan and containing a 42-foot-long (13-metre) oak table shuffle board. Excavations of this enclosure in the 1980s revealed an eighteenth-century patterned garden made using the different textures and colours of sea shells, lime mortar, brick dust, coal dust, white sand, orange sand and grass. Today's pattern is an impression of how the original garden must have looked.

The Orchard Garden at Tredegar House

Lakeside walk with redwoods and rhododendrons ▸

TRETOWER COURT

Wales is blessed with a wealth of gardens representing different periods of garden history, particularly gardens from the eighteenth-century Picturesque Garden Landscape movement, the Victorian era and the Edwardian Arts & Crafts period. There are also some gardens that can date their origins back to the time of the Stuarts and even the late Tudor period. However, relatively few, if any, truly original medieval gardens survive in modern-day Wales, which is why the work carried out by CADW at Tretower Court, near Crickhowell on the edge of the Black Mountains, is so important. For here, in the grounds of this fifteenth-century fortified manor house and castle, is a medieval garden, or at least a recreation of a medieval garden, which has been designed and planted as authentically as possible to illustrate the typical garden of a wealthy commoner in the mid-fifteenth century.

The garden was first laid out by CADW in 1991 and has been created to reflect both the garden style of the fifteenth century and the medieval owner of Tretower Court, Sir Roger Vaughan. It includes, for example, a tunnel arbour that has been planted with the white rose *Rosa x alba* 'Alba Semiplena'; Sir Roger was a prominent Yorkist and this rose was the Yorkist symbol. ▸

Tretower Court Garden, with plants that were available in the fifteenth century

Rosa gallica 'Versicolor' ▸

◀ The design, structure and planting are all authentic and typical of gardens of this status at the time. Only plants available in the fifteenth century have been used and they all had multiple uses. They were ornamental and they were symbolic, such as the Madonna lily *Lilium candidum* – the emblem of the Virgin Mary. Some ornamental plants could be eaten or used as herbs and spices in cooking. Others were medicinal or used as dyes, perfume, or for strewing on the floor to hide the pungent smells of everyday medieval life.

Vines such as *Vitis vinifera* 'Madeleine Angevine', honeysuckle, *Rosa mundi* and *Rosa gallica* 'Versicolor', which are all documented to have been widely grown in fifteenth-century gardens, are also prominent here.

There is a chequerboard patterned garden with beds planted with flowers that figured prominently in medieval pleasure gardens, such as lilies, irises, peonies, columbines, pinks and violets, and a dripping fountain, which is typical of medieval gardens of high status. Completing this excellent medieval recreation is a 'herber' – a garden room enclosed by trelliswork and designed for quiet contemplation, a lawn planted with medlar, quince, pear and mulberry and a turf seat – all accurate features of the era.

Tunnel arbour with vines at Tretower Court

VEDDW HOUSE

Considering one of the owners and creator of this garden has made a name for herself for being 'bad tempered', the gardens at Veddw House are, in the main, remarkably relaxed and full of charm, wit and reflectiveness. Anne Wareham, along with award-winning garden photographer Charles Hawes, has been gardening here since 1987, in an amphitheatre among the wooded hills that rise majestically above the Wye Valley and the ancient border with England.

First impression of Veddw, as one enters this 2-acre (0.8-hectare) garden from the car park above, is of a series of garden rooms bordered by yew and two-tone beech hedges. Nothing unusual in that, you may say, but a second and perhaps more careful survey will reveal that no two hedges are the same. Several rhythmically rise and fall like the back of a prehistoric creature crossing Loch Ness, others plunge abruptly to offer a sudden reveal of the garden beyond and some are so sharply angled they are reminiscent of chainsaw teeth, ferocious in their intent, but cleverly softened by the curves of nearby yew topiary cones and the muted colours of elymus grasses and pink-flowering persicaria.

When you eventually immerse yourself within this structural labyrinth, you are drawn around the garden by the constant changes of styles and little brain-teasers encountered along the way. 'Wherever you go there is always somewhere else to go ', says Anne; she is right, of course, but you could add and something else to muse upon. ▸

Hedges rhythmically rise and fall

◀ From the headstones in the Wild Garden to carefully placed seating with backs that mimic the sinuous outlines of the hedging, this garden constantly offers ideas, some practical, some that need to be unlocked like a riddle.

Borders full of interesting plants (and deliberately left weeds, spared because they offer something to the whole), a vegetable garden enclosed by old scented roses, pergolas draped with purple-leaved vines, banks of rough-leaved villosa hydrangeas and a box parterre, which traces the field boundaries from an 1848 tithe map, all add to this remarkable garden.

Just a final word of warning – when you visit Veddw (and visit you must), do not tell Anne Wareham that you think her garden lovely, or you just might find yourself accused of being provocative. Lovely it may be, but rather than generic compliments, what Anne would much rather hear is an honest appraisal of her garden. Offer your thoughtful critique with enthusiasm and you will undoubtedly have her undivided attention!

◀ 'Wherever you go there is always somewhere else to go'

Lily pool borders

WHIMBLE GARDEN AND NURSERY

Tucked away on the south-facing slopes of the beautiful Radnorshire Hills, this richly planted garden is an absolute delight, particularly in high summer. Specialising in unusual herbaceous plants and climbers (many of which are for sale in the adjoining nursery), everything is carefully chosen for beauty, colour and form.

In the main garden, a yew walk created in 1998 leads to a series of garden rooms, including a box-edged parterre, which is divided into colour-themed quadrants densely planted with bulbs, perennials and some unusual annuals. Together, these produce a subtle tapestry of colour throughout the growing season.

The centrepiece of the Gemini Garden, created in 2009, is a brace of raised ponds constructed from Radnorshire slate and topped with warm brown-planked timber. The planting is minimalist and mainly contained in large pots using a blue, white and yellow colour scheme. Close by, a flowery mead in pastel shades and a bed of Dianthus cultivars provides the perfect contrast.

In the Fernery and Woodpecker Garden, climbers and bamboos planted around natural ponds offer shade and shelter to a fine collection of ferns, while a nearby seat provides dramatic views of the mountains. ▸

Parterre in midsummer

◂ Perhaps the most unusual feature in the garden is a metal sculpture in the form of a ruined church. It was constructed in 1999 and is now bedecked with purple-leaved vines, scented roses and rare clematis. Wall germander *Teucrium chamaedrys* surrounds the outside walls, which have box buttresses.

In the Lavender Garden, planted circles of 'Hidcote' lavender are combined with tubs planted with bulbs in spring, followed by complementary tender perennials. Here, an arbour clothed with Rosa 'Evangeline' and Rosa 'Sombreuil' leads to four square beds full of ornamental grasses, which provide form and interest well into late autumn and winter.

From here, a gate cut through beech hedges planted in 2001 opens into two enclosures, one with clipped box topiary and beds of annual cornfield flower mix, the other containing a swallow house where views open out to the meadow beyond. It is cut for hay and is gradually being brought back to a traditional meadow. Paths cut through the grass lead through an archway and on to a nuttery, young woodlands and even the odd wooden boat or two! At the far end of the garden is the 'Toposcope', from which vistas extend eastwards to the borderland with England and Hergest Ridge and westwards to the verdant slopes of Radnor Forest.

The boat in the nature reserve

❁ WYNDCLIFFE COURT

This important Monmouthshire Historic Grade II Listed Arts & Crafts garden was designed by Henry Avray Tipping for Wyndcliffe owner Charles Clay before the First World War and completed in 1922.

Tipping's garden designs were very popular around this period. His ability to blend the formality and crisp lines of the Arts & Crafts style with the wildness of natural landscapes, and woodland in particular, is probably seen at its best at Wyndcliffe. Here, red-sand-stone-bordered terraces cascade away from the house and down a south-facing slope towards a woodland dell and pond, where meandering, shady paths lead to far-reaching views across the Severn estuary.

The terrace nearest the house is broad and paved in local stone; two shallow flights of steps lead from here down to the topiary terrace, which has a semi-circular pool complete with an elegant trickling dolphin fountain, yew topiary and rectangular beds planted in the main with annuals, bulbs and herbaceous material. In late summer, beautiful swathes of Japanese anemones soften the stonework; however, it is the topiary drums or 'penny buns' that always command attention, their once perfect lines now gracefully relaxing after almost a century of clipping. It is true to say that Wyndcliffe is perhaps not maintained today to the exacting standards of the 1920s and '30s. ▶

Productive garden surrounded by ornamental shrubs

The sunken garden ▶

Nonetheless, both the infrastructure and the planting is still strong enough to convey an atmosphere of those bygone days, so often perceived as being the very zenith of English garden design. Below the terracing, the smooth green surface of a bowling green acts as the interface between formality and the woodland beyond.

To the west of the garden lies a delightful sunken garden. At its centre is a rectangular stone-bordered lily pond, complete with bathing stone maiden and surrounded by large-leaved bergenias, which climb up the banks to meet borders of shrubs revelling in this sheltered environment. Positioned perfectly on its south-west corner is a charming stone-built summerhouse. The surprise comes as one ascends to its viewing platform, where vistas open up not only of the immediate sunken garden, but back towards the house and its formal terracing, and then further westwards to a large walled vegetable and cutting garden surrounded by a fine collection of ornamental trees and shrubs.

The current owners of Wyndcliffe are both artists and entrepreneurs, and as well as embarking on a worthy garden restoration, they also display an intriguing array of sculpture within its grounds.

Wyndcliffe Court with topiary terraces